Tales & Truths

"It's hard to imagine a better way to learn about the evolution of wilderness fire suppression than to read Bill Moody's *Tales and Truths: 60 Years of Firefighting from Hell's Canyon to the Amazon*. The memoir not only describes efforts to save incalculable millions of acres of forest, it brings the man's wisdom and influence into clearer focus for anyone who's met or worked with Moody. The compelling authenticity of the book is a result of meticulously detailed personal notes the author kept over the years. And those who remember the first glory days of the North Cascades Smokejumper Base, which Moody managed for seventeen years, will recognize the names of fire fighters who've advanced in the ranks or blended into other careers and communities, and some who've died in action. This book gives them all tribute."

~Susan Lagsdin

Tales & Truths

60 Years of Firefighting
From Hells Canyon to the Amazon

Bill Moody

ᘒᘒ

Methow Press
Twisp, Washington 98856

Published by Methow Press

P.O. Box 1213, Twisp, WA 98856
https://www.methowpress.com

Printed in the United States of America

ISBN 13: 978-1-970777-40-6

Cover image, "Bill Moody, Spotter," by Brad Hughes, courtesy the Bill Moody collection. Other photos also courtesy the Moody collection. Used by permission. Cover graphics design by Methow Press.

This book is dedicated to Francis B. "Pappy" Lufkin—
pioneer smokejumper, my mentor, and my friend—and to the
"brotherhood of smokejumpers."

Contents

Part 1
60 Years of Firefighting

Introduction

It was my first smokejumper fire, July 13, 1957. The chute opened. There below me was the deepest canyon in the United States, Hells Canyon. Sixty years later I was flying in a King Air 350 in front of a 747 airtanker on a low-level water drop over the Amazon forests of Bolivia.

What was to be a "get yourself through college" job ended up being an exciting and challenging sixty-plus-year wildland firefighting career, thirty-three of those seasons as a U.S. Forest Service smokejumper parachuting to fires throughout the western United States, plus two exhibition jumps in Russia. Smokejumping would prove to be the gateway, as they say, to more opportunities and exciting adventures related to wildland firefighting—four decades as an Air Attack (manager of aircraft over a fire incident), sixteen years as a fire operations specialist consultant/instructor with the 747 Supertanker (airtanker) program, and three years as a fire consultant and trainer of Mongolian firefighters—and one hell of a lot of personal growth.

Throughout my life I have been blessed by people in my life— teachers, friends, professional associates, co-workers, a personal hero, and mentors—who, through their suggestions, endorsement, encouragement, and mentoring, "tempted me" with interesting, exciting, and challenging opportunities out of my comfort zone. With curiosity, anxiety, and fear, I accepted them.

Most of them weren't planned but were the result of a timely call or contact. Words of encouragement and confidence inspired me enough to pursue those opportunities. Looking back, most of them came out of the blue, totally unexpectedly. I am convinced it was all a "God thing."

Several times over the past twenty years I have been encouraged to write a book about my career as a wildland firefighter—difficult jumps, challenging fires, difficult para-rescues, my broken femur, a one-on-one with Benjamin Netanyahu in Israel, the presentation at the Smithsonian Air and Space Museum with Francis Lufkin, jumping with the Russians in East Siberia, training Mongolian firefighters in the land of Genghis Khan, and many more adventures.

This volume is a collection of memoirs taken from my work diaries, my jump logs, previously published articles for the National Smokejumper Association or U.S. Forest Service, and my recollection of the details of what happened.

Becoming a Smokejumper

Born in 1939, the year of the "Parachute Experimental Project," I could not have known that the success of the parachute experiment would provide me with a career opportunity eighteen years later, an initial career in fire that would last from 1957 to 1989. But those experimental years laid a foundation for me to become a smokejumper.

The Seed Is Sown

In 1944, at the age of five, I met the person who became my hero, and who inspired me to become a "Forest Service paratrooper"—a smokejumper. That person was my cousin's husband, then-Lieutenant Bob Hammerquist.

Bob was a newly-commissioned officer and paratrooper in the 17th Airborne Division, soon to be deployed to Europe. Bob fought in The Battle of the Bulge, for which he received a Purple Heart. After recovering, a few months later, he parachuted as part of Operation Varsity into Germany, where he once again was wounded after leading his men to secure a key bridge on the Issel River. For his heroic action he was awarded the Distinguished Service Cross.

Bob went on to serve in Korea, Vietnam, and the Pentagon, retiring as a Colonel. What an impressive man, a paratrooper. Wow! Bob was my lifelong hero.

Growing Up Years

Growing up in western Washington, I was a Cub and Boy Scout, loved to fish, and played the traditional sports. In high school I played varsity football and competed in track. From ages nine to thirteen, I was a paperboy for the Everett *Daily Herald*, *Seattle Times*, and the Wallingford weekly newspaper. I also was a bag boy at Food Giant and worked for my parents at our Apex Cleaners shop in the Wallingford District of Seattle.

I spent several summers on my aunt and uncle's ranch in Montana—a quasi "junior ranch hand," with time out for trout fishing and shooting magpies and gophers.

A Fire Career Set in Motion

On a whim, my foster brother Ron Loney convinced me to spend the summer between our junior and senior years in high school working for a sawmill in central Oregon. Ron's brother-in-law would help us get the job at the sawmill. We were set and headed for Gilchrist, Oregon, in July 1956. As unpaid volunteers we hung out at the Gilchrist sawmill. There we learned how to sort, grade, and stack green lumber as it came off the saw on a conveyor belt, called "the green chain." This experience would lead to a paid position in an independent sawmill—one of the "gyppo" mills—where we were assigned to the night green chain crew.

After two miserable weeks on the green chain, while playing softball with a Forest Service fire crew, we learned that the Crescent Ranger District of the Deschutes National Forest had two vacancies on their tree-pruning and fire crew. We applied, even though I had only just turned seventeen. On my application I stated that I was eighteen—a lie I lived with until my firefighter retirement papers were signed in 1989. Ranger Hardman hired us for $1.50 an hour.

My fire career was launched. Our first experience with fighting wildfire happened on our first day on the fire crew.

The next couple of weeks were committed to fire training, pruning ponderosa and sugar pine, and fighting a couple of small fires. That first year we learned a lot about fighting fire, and we were introduced to smokejumpers.

A lightning storm ignited a small fire on a ridge several miles from the nearest road. Our foreman drove the crew to a vantage point where we could observe two Siskiyou jumpers jump—pretty cool! We learned that smokejumpers were the elite of the wildland firefighters.

Meanwhile, our classmate and buddy Jack McKay, working on the Snoqualmie National Forest fire crew, met some Okanogan Aerial Project jumpers while working on the McAllister fire in the North Cascades. He was quite impressed with the jumpers and felt he needed to learn more about smokejumpers, maybe even become one the next summer.

Experience gained on the fire crew in 1956 set in motion a sixty-year firefighting career. It qualified me for a smokejumper position in 1957, and it would lead to a temporary Air Attack Officer assignment, and eventually to the Base Manager position. This, in turn, after retirement, landed me a consulting position and Chief of Fire Operations for the 747 airtanker program.

All that came out of one wild whim to go work at an Oregon sawmill in 1956.

During my senior year at Lincoln High School in Seattle, Jack suggested that, after graduation, he, Ron, and I apply for smokejumping at the Okanogan Aerial Project located at Winthrop, Washington. Other than our brief encounter with smokejumpers in 1956, all we knew about smokejumping came from watching the 1952 film inspired by the 1949 tragic Mann Gulch Fire, *Red Skies of Montana*.

We concluded that parachuting looked like an exciting way to get to a fire, and it probably paid well—and my paratrooper cousin would be proud of me.

During Christmas break we drove to the Okanogan Aerial Project Base near Winthrop. We introduced ourselves to the base overhead—the staff in charge—and expressed our interest in employment and picked up an application.

Little did we know that the Okanogan Aerial Project Base was the site of the 1939 Smokejumper Experiment Project or that our boss would be 1939 Smokejumper Experiment Project pioneer Francis B. Lufkin. Or that the Okanogan Aerial Project served the "toughest" smokejumper region in the United States, the North Cascades, and that rookie smokejumper training was an arduous four-week program.

We were hired that winter while still in high school and were scheduled to start the four-week training course in June 1957, two weeks after I turned eighteen and graduated from high school. During the next several weeks we were getting into shape for what we understood would be a grueling four-week training program—and it was!

Rookie Smokejumper Training 1957

The week before reporting for smokejumper training, Jack and I thought it would be good to have experienced an airplane ride. We selected Bellevue Airfield (no longer there) along what is now I-90. All we could afford was a ten-minute ride in a single-engine Cessna. Pretty exciting, but not as exciting as our next ascent in a smokejumper jump plane—a one-way ride up, with a 2,000-foot parachute ride down.

Two weeks after graduating from high school, Jack, Ron, and I (and nineteen other candidates) reported to the Okanogan Aerial Project (now North Cascades Smokejumper Base) for rookie smokejumper training, a four-week intense course in mountain parachuting and fire operations. The pay was $1.79 an hour, with overtime at the same rate. (In the early 1970s there was a major adjustment to the pay structure—overtime paid at time-and-a-half, hazard pay for fighting an uncontrolled fire, hazard pay for being in the aircraft during low-level cargo drops, and a few others.) There were deductions for sleeping in the Forest Service bunkhouse and for meals in the Forest Service mess hall—but at least the food was great, and all you could eat! I would clear about $2,000-2500 for a summer's work—just enough to pay for a year at the University of Washington and later at Central Washington University.

The training was arduous, including two hours a day of physical training (PT). Being a high school football player and miler on the track team paid off, since running was a big part of our PT. The balance of our daily routine consisted of parachute manipulation and parachute emergencies, jumping from the jump tower to simulate exits from an airplane, letdown procedures after landing in a tree, exiting from the aircraft, tree climbing with lineman spurs, fire behavior, first aid, and pump, chainsaw, and cross-cut saw training, and more.

During the next two weeks we made seven parachute jumps under increasingly difficult conditions. The first two weeks were physically exhausting, and the next two weeks of live jumps were psychologically exhausting—fighting fear, nervousness, and anxiety, and questioning "What in hell am I doing here?"

The aircraft we jumped from during our training was the home-based Noorduyn Norseman and a contract Twin Beech. Both carried four jumpers and a spotter (the "jump master"). Normally, two jumpers would jump on each pass over the exit point, upwind of the landing area (the "jump spot"). The landing area for the first three jumps was the Bear Creek jump spot—Cougar Flat, south of Cougar Lake, just east of Bowen Mountain. Aircraft exits were made from 2,000 feet above ground elevation at 75 and 80 mph.

The first two weeks of ground training conditioned me to follow the jump protocols without really thinking: snap the static line on the anchor cable near the exit door, position yourself in the jump exit door or behind the jumper in the door, wait for the spotter to slap me on the shoulder (to signal me to jump), exit, strive to attain a vertical body position, check the chute after it opens, and maneuver to the jump spot. Failure to attain vertical exit position—i.e., head down, on your side, tumbling, etc.—would result in a very hard opening, possibly a parachute malfunction, parachute lines/riser scraping your neck, harness abrasions on your clavicles, loss of helmet, or even being knocked unconscious... all adding to the fear. An incentive to get a vertical body position. Easier said than done!

By the third and fourth jump I was a bit more coherent; by the sixth and seventh I kind of had it together and was more confident. I never thought of quitting, although some did. Social pressure kept me in the program. *If I can only make it through the fire season, it will be over and I can "retire."* With each jump, seven total, I grew more confident, and the fears and doubts diminished but were still there.

Now, the real test: jumping to a fire under normal operational conditions in the North Cascades, or wherever the call led. Over the years, even with several hundred jumps, I learned to "respect the environment" I was in—take every jump seriously, take nothing for granted—and say a short prayer while in the door before exiting.

Baptism Over Hells Canyon

Upon completing the four weeks of training, we drew lots for a position on the jump list, the order in which you would be assigned to fire duty. I drew Number 3. The following morning, after the rookie graduation bash, I and five other "hung-over" jumpers flew to our spike base at La Grande, Oregon. The Noorduyn Norseman, piloted by veteran pilot Wally Tower, chugged along at a blistering cruise speed of 130 mph, landing in La Grande about two hours later.

A contract Twin Beech jump plane was waiting for us when we arrived at La Grande. The first two jumpers on the jump list suited up and were soon on their way to a fire near Hells Canyon, the deepest canyon in North America.

It seemed like an eternity before the plane returned, minus two jumpers. We were anxious to hear about their jump and what might await us. The spotter reported that the jumpers had a small jump spot, a tough jump! It was windy, and they nearly missed the spot. Not encouraging news for a rookie jumper on my first fire jump.

After refueling we boarded the plane: Moody, Ron Roberts, Ray Casey, and Tim Wapato, the only experienced jumper. After a short briefing we headed for the Squaw Creek Fire on the Imnaha-Snake Ranger District of the Wallowa-Whitman National Forest. The location was in Hells Canyon, east of McGraw Lookout, west of the Snake River, on the Oregon-Idaho border.

I quickly dozed off. Waking me up from a nervous sleep, the plane made a circle over the fire.

I looked out the jump exit door and saw the fire, rocky cliffs, then the Snake River below the fire. Thoughts went through my mind. *Where is the spotter going to put us? Hopefully in that small opening surrounded by trees. What if I miss the spot and I land in the river? Sure a lot of steep, rocky terrain surrounding the jump spot. Our jump training jump spots were nothing like this. Maybe the spotter will call it off due to too much wind.*

Convinced that we were going to jump this fire, I finally pulled myself together mentally and prepared for the jump.

The fire, about two acres in size, was indeed in steep, rocky terrain. The jump spot was a small, flat bench covered with scattered large ponderosa pine. Minutes later jump partner Ron Roberts and I exited. After a rapid, windy descent I bagged a tall tree and proceeded with a 125-foot letdown from the old-growth ponderosa. We gathered our cargo, and it was "balls to the wall" constructing a fireline.

It sank in. *So this is what smokejumping is all about.* The fire spread was slow, as part of the fire had burned out on its own. It would take two days to put the fire out.

For dinner the Ranger District dropped us breaded veal cutlets, mashed potatoes, and apple pie. Two days later, we started the fifteen-mile hike out, up to McGraw Lookout, where we overnighted. Then down to the Imnaha-Snake Ranger Station and a chicken dinner with the ranger and his wife.

What an initiation to smokejumping! It never got better than this.

During my first year I made five fire jumps. After the Hells Canyon Fire I made three more fire jumps in the Blue Mountains of northeast Oregon. My fifth fire jump was on the Okanogan National Forest, nine miles up Wolf Creek, west of Winthrop.

The hook was set. I made it through my rookie year without an injury, the pay was relatively good, and I made enough to cover my freshman year at the University of Washington. The job was very exciting, and I hoped my paratrooper hero would be very proud of me, which he was.

As I reflected on the summer smokejumping experience, I realized that it was more than the $2,000 I made or the five successful fire jumps. It was about what I gained personally— self-confidence, the ability to meet difficult physical and psychological challenges, a great increase in physical strength, and a deep sense of belonging to a very special fraternity: *smokejumpers.* I would return for another fire season in 1958.

No Longer a Rookie

In June of 1958 I returned to NCSB for my second season, no longer a rookie.

In contrast to the previous fire season, the 1958 season started out hot and dry with lightning storms. It proved not only a very active fire season, but a tragic one.

I finished my freshman year at the University of Washington with average grades and an undeclared major. An Advanced First Aid course I took would end up landing me the rookie training first-aid instructor's position for the new recruits scheduled to report in June. The 1957 PT instructor was not returning. I volunteered for that position as well. Lufkin approved, and now I had four hours instructing in weeks one and two, with twenty-two rookies to train.

Immediately after we veteran jumpers completed a three-day, two-jump refresher course, we all started jumping lightning-caused fires on the Okanogan National Forest. In addition to the rookie jumpers, we also had a new smokejumper pilot to break in, Bob Cavanaugh. Bob was a WWII Navy carrier pilot. On Sunday, June 22, several of us watched the WWII documentary *Victory at Sea*. Bob narrated the action—action he knew first-hand. The following day, Bob, along with three jumpers, would perish in a fiery plane crash on Eight Mile Ridge north of Winthrop.

The Eight Mile Ridge Disaster

The 23rd of June was hot with thunderstorms building throughout the day. Around noon we started getting lightning-caused fires and requests for smokejumpers. We dropped jumpers on the east side of the Okanogan National Forest and five jumpers north of Winthrop on Eight Mile Ridge. By mid-afternoon it was 105 degrees F. Lightning continued, and as more fires were reported we were about out of jumpers.

The jumpers on the Eight Mile Ridge Fire reported the fire to be about five acres. Reinforcements were requested. Twenty of our rookies, under Elmer Neufeld's leadership, were dispatched to assist.

Two more fires were reported on the Winthrop Ranger District. Supervisory Smokejumper Chet Putnam and I were dispatched to the Andrews Creek Fire while Jim Wescott and Roy Percival were assigned to the Disaster Creek Fire near Black Lake on the Winthrop Ranger District. Our spotter was Senior Supervisory Smokejumper and head trainer Gus Hendrickson. This would be the last time we saw Gus. In a couple of hours he would die in a fatal plane crash a few miles away.

As we arrived over the Andrews Creek Fire, the air was very unstable, with lightning in the area. The wind velocity for jumping was marginal. To compensate for the wind and parachute drift distance, the jump was made from 800 feet above the landing area instead of the standard 1,200 to 1,500 feet. Upon exit we found ourselves in a downdraft. It took me only about eight seconds from exit to landing in a short fir tree. The cargo was dropped and gathered, and the small fire was quickly contained. We hiked to the road in the dark. It wasn't until we reached the Winthrop Cafe, on the way to the base, that we learned that the jump plane, with three jumpers on board, had crashed on Eight Mile Ridge—a victim of the same unstable, turbulent air that challenged our jump.

The plane crash killed three jumpers: Keith Hendrickson, Senior Supervisory Smokejumper ; Gerald Helmer, Squad-leader trainee; and Bob Carlman, Winthrop Ranger District Forester and qualified smokejumper who trained in 1957; plus pilot Bob Cavanaugh. This was one of the most tragic and emotional experiences of my life. The rookies had only completed one week of training. Many of the rookies thought seriously about quitting—but none did.

Rookie training continued. A few days later we were back to jumping fires in the Cascades.

Sixty years after the fatal plane crash, I was contacted by the children of pilot Bob Cavanaugh, asking if I knew their father, and if so, could I tell them about him. I responded with a letter to the family and wrote a feature article in the National Smokejumper Association quarterly magazine, "Tell Us About Our Father." A full reprint of the article is included in Part 2 of this volume.

After the fatalities, I took on additional rookie training duties. As predicted, the 1958 fire season was very busy, both out of NCSB and our satellite base in La Grande, Oregon. Particularly hard hit was the Okanogan National Forest, the North Cascades, and Lake Chelan. The jump season didn't end until October. During the season I made twelve fire jumps. A couple of the more memorable jumps are briefly described in the chapter titled, "Memorable Jumps."

1959 and 1960 Fire Seasons

In early 1959 I talked to Francis Lufkin about going to Silver City, New Mexico, in the spring as a member of the inter-base jumper crew assigned to the Gila National Forest. Jumpers usually got several jumps, and it was a great adventure. To do so, I would have to drop out of college for the spring quarter. Lufkin wisely counseled me that I should stay on track in college, without an interruption, and complete my degree. Had I actually dropped out of college for the spring quarter, it would have drastically changed my "life timeline," career, and many future opportunities. Thanks, Francis!

The 1959 fire season was very slow, with only a few jumper fires in the North Cascades and eastern Washington. Fires in Northeast Oregon provided most of our jump activity. A few of my notable fires from that season are also included in "Memorable Jumps."

The 1960 fire season was very hot and dry, but there were again relatively few smokejumper fires in Washington State. Northeast Oregon, on the other hand, was hit with major lightning storms and fires, which kept us busy throughout the summer. Our La Grande satellite base, which was staffed from the 4th of July, was a major hub of activity.

Sharing the Smokejumper Life

The most memorable event of 1960 was my marriage to a wheat-rancher's daughter from Odessa, Washington—Sandy Sackmann. We met in 1959 at Central Washington College and married in December 1960, between college quarters. She became a "smokejumper's wife," and an integral part of the smokejumper culture. From now on any decisions regarding a "smokejumper future" would require her input and approval. Would I be a "full-time teacher," evolve through the smokejumper career ranks, or both?

In June 1961, I completed my BA Education degree in social studies with a geography major. I was hired by the Wenatchee School District, where I had done my student teaching the previous year, to teach geography and math and to coach track and football at Pioneer Junior High School. Sandy worked as the secretary to the Wenatchee Junior College president and continued with her college education in elementary education.

Military Exemption

Throughout my adult life I have wrestled with the fact that I did not serve in the military. In 1957, at age eighteen and a high school graduate, I registered for the draft with the Seattle Selective Service Board. The year 1957 was between the Korean War and the Vietnam War. It was a period of what seemed to be low draft call-up.

Although I didn't agree with the Vietnam War, I was a patriot. I certainly would have served had I been drafted. By the time of the heavy draft call-up in the late 1960s I was married, a public-school teacher, and a Supervisory Smokejumper . I would go on to a thirty-three-year jump career and thirty-five years as an Air Attack Officer. Yet I still have mixed emotions about having not served and missing the military experience.

Balancing Two Careers

From 1961 to 1969 I had two careers, teaching junior and senior high school in Wenatchee and being a Supervisory Smokejumper at the re-christened North Cascades Smokejumper Base (NCSB) and at our satellite base in La Grande. During these years I generally worked at the jump base from early June until the first week of September, before returning to Wenatchee to teach school. If the fall fire season was busy, I often worked weekends at NCSB. I was laying a foundation for becoming a full-time smokejumper, eventually becoming the Base Manager. That foundation included managing a small base operation by myself.

That opportunity came in 1961 when I was detailed to La Grande to assist Supervisory Smokejumper Hal Weinmann. It was a period of high fire activity caused by daily lightning storms occurring on the Wallowa-Whitman, Umatilla, and Malheur National Forests. In addition to North Cascades jumpers, there were several jumpers from other bases. Due to family circumstances, Hal could only be at the base occasionally for short periods of time. I was essentially running a very busy jumper operation by myself.

Hal, in spite of being there just part-time, mentored me through this intense period. My duties included general crew logistics, managing the jump list and spotting assignments, spotting, packing parachutes, and preparing fire packs/cargo for dropping—and all the paperwork required when managing a base operation. For me it was almost a 24/7 operation, but what a valuable experience.

In 1963 I went back to Central Washington University (fall through spring) to pursue a Master's degree. My Master's thesis was titled, "Fighting Forest Fires in the Western United States," a filmstrip and manual designed for middle school

18

teachers for teaching about methods of controlling wildfires in the Western United States. After receiving my Master's in June 1964, I returned to NCSB.

During the 1964 and 1965 fire seasons I was back in La Grande, this time in charge of La Grande Satellite Base for the summer. Although the fire seasons were moderately active, I gained a great deal of experience managing not only NCSB jumpers but also booster crew—jumpers borrowed from other bases to boost the size of our crew. Great experience!

A Mae West over Jack Creek

The fall of 1964 turned warm and dry. After heading up the La Grande satellite base for the summer I returned to NCSB to finish out the fire season. I made nine smokejumps and a ground attack from September 9th to November 2nd. The fall fire season came to an abrupt end the eve of November 2 when multiple escaped hunter warming fires, scattered over the Okanogan National Forest, were extinguished by a six-inch snow.

During my 33 years of jumping I never had a "significant" parachute malfunction—that is, not until my jump to the Jack Creek Fire, Okanogan National Forest, Twisp Ranger District, on November 2.

The morning was overcast, temperatures were in the teens, and there was already a pretty stiff morning wind. By mid-morning Okanogan Fire Dispatch had reported three fires, likely early-morning hunter warming fires that weren't put out. Two of those fires were on the Twisp Ranger District, and Ranger Graw wanted the jumpers to put them out.

The jumper request was placed. The jump plane was a U.S. Forest Service Twin Beech. Spotter Tony Percival and jumpers John Lester, Burr Satterfield, Terry McCabe, and I were the crew. The air was very turbulent as we navigated toward the

Loup Loup Ski Bowl to take action on the first fire, the Little Buck Mountain Fire. The wind-drift indicators verified what we thought the jump conditions would be—marginal jump winds with gusts. After adjustments to the plane's flight path, jumpers Lester and Satterfield exited to attack this fire. Overcome by the wind, the jumpers landed coming in backwards. Lester's helmeted head struck a stump, splitting his helmet and knocking him out for a few minutes. The fire tool pack was dropped, and we proceeded to the next fire, the Jack Creek Fire. The fire was about a tenth of an acre.

The general "jump conditions" were the same over Jack Creek as they were where we dropped Lester and Satterfield—turbulent with marginal winds. Jump partner Terry McCabe and I were in for an exciting jump! The drift streamers confirmed the conditions—wind around 15-20 mph with gusts. We would exit the plane at around 1,000 feet above ground level, about a quarter of a mile or more from the selected landing area. As my 28-foot FS-2 chute, with no deployment bag, opened, it malfunctioned, allowing half of the chute shroud-lines to loop over the canopy, resulting in what looks like a big bra—thus the term a "Mae West."

The partially-open canopy results in a fast descent, two to three times the normal rate, and you lose directional control. My immediate response was to deploy my reserve (emergency) chute as per our training—throw/push the reserve away from you, allowing it to inflate. Once the reserve chute inflated, I would be able descend under both the compromised main and reserve. Unfortunately, however, as I threw the reserve away from me, the wind blew it right back on me. If I had been able to turn the chute and drift with the wind, I probably would have ended up in Douglas County.

Between attempts to inflate the reserve, I glanced up to check on Terry. He was several hundred feet above me. After my fourth attempt, and as I was about to slam into a pine tree, the chute fully opened and I landed softly on a big rotten log. Had I landed on the ground without the aid of the reserve chute, I probably would have sustained a serious injury.

After retrieving the wind-scattered cargo, we got to work firelining and mopping up the fire. We settled in for a cold night in our paper sleeping bags. That night it snowed five inches on the fire—and on us! The fire season was over.

The Dual Career Continues Through the '60s

In early December 1964, I joined my wife in Wenatchee, where she was finishing her student teaching. From January through spring, we both went back to college, where Sandy finished her degree and I took postgraduate "enrichment" courses.

Around this time the Wenatchee National Forest contacted me regarding a position associated with a Job Corp center being established, either at Leavenworth or Moses Lake. I was not interested.

In 1965 I returned for another season of smokejumping, followed by another year in the classroom. By then Sandy and I thought our course was set—teaching in the fall-spring, smokejumping in the summer. Sandy had a fourth-grade teaching job at Columbia Elementary School in Wenatchee and I returned to Pioneer Junior High.

In 1966 I moved to Wenatchee High School, where I taught Contemporary World Problems and coached JV football and varsity track distance-runners. By 1967 I became Social Studies Co-Department Head.

The annual migration to the Methow for fire season continued through the '60s, but the 1968 season would be different. Sandy was pregnant with our first child, Mary Kay, due at the beginning of the jump season. We would be staying in a small trailer house located on the west side of the jump base airport.

The second week of June, as soon as school was out, I moved from our newly-built house in East Wenatchee to our summer quarters in the Methow. Sandy followed on June 11th to get the trailer "livable." Her due date wasn't until late June.

After a full day of cleaning the trailer, she felt a rush of water run down her leg—could it be her water breaking three weeks early?

I consulted with jumper Bob Veitch, a med student. Bob advised us to get her to her doctor in Wenatchee ASAP. At 2300 hours we left for Wenatchee with an emergency gas stop in Chelan. Mary Kay was born the following morning at 0815.

An interesting note: After Francis Lufkin retired, he and Lola moved to Bellingham, Washington. Bob Veitch, now a doctor in Bellingham, became the Lufkin family doctor.

The Teaching Degree Pays Off

Having a teaching degree—and with six years of teaching under my belt by 1969—would prove to be a tremendous help in establishing my future career. It would lead to numerous career opportunities that I wouldn't have had otherwise—like being selected as Base Manager in 1972. It also led to instructing regional- and national-level courses, Fire and Aviation-related course development projects, and assignments to special projects, including being selected for the U.S.-Soviet Technical Exchange Program in 1976.

How About Becoming a Full-Time Smokejumper?

I began to consider a full-time smokejumper foreman position, perhaps even the Base Manager position after Francis retired. I asked Francis how competitive I would be and what my chances were of being selected to replace him. His reply was positive, with no guarantees, and said that it would no doubt be very competitive—but he would support me by providing training and work experience I would need to be competitive. He was the mentor I needed.

This would be a major decision for our family—to give up a new home in East Wenatchee, a dream teaching job, department head and coaching positions at Wenatchee High School, and all for less money with no guarantee of becoming the next Base Manager.

In the spring of 1969, after six years of teaching, I submitted my resignation. We sold our house, contracted our previous builder to build us a new house in Twisp, and loaded up Sandy and daughter Mary Kay. It was "Methow or Bust!"

A Career-Building Fire Season

Throughout one's career there are key mentors, opportunities, or experiences. Although I had multiple mentors over my career, one stands out: Francis B. Lufkin, pioneer smokejumper and now my boss. How fortunate I was to have Francis as my mentor, a man of the highest integrity and greatly respected by all who knew him. I had the privilege of working under Francis from 1957 until I replaced him as Base Manager in 1972.

In the October 2022 National Smokejumper Association quarterly magazine, I published an article about Francis, the full text of which is included in Part 2 of this volume. The section that follows is a summary.

"Pappy"

The North Cascades Smokejumper Base legacy can be attributed to Francis B. Lufkin, a man for the times. He was a pioneer from the 1939 Parachute Experiment Project, who in 1940, along with fellow pioneer Glen Smith, would make the first jumps to a wildfire in the Pacific Northwest Region of the U.S. Forest Service.

Francis moved to the Methow Valley as a teenager in 1929, graduated from Winthrop High School in 1933, and married his wife, Lola, in 1937. In 1939 he applied for and was selected to be a participant in the U.S. Forest Service Parachute Experiment Project. He was hired as a tree climber to retrieve parachutes when jumpers landed in trees.

On the last day of the Parachute Experiment he was dared to make a jump, and that started a thirty-three year smokejumper career at what is now the North Cascades Smokejumper Base.

In 1957, I was selected to be a smokejumper at NCSB, where I would be working for a pioneer legend. What a privilege to have worked under his leadership and mentorship for sixteen years. Few people have had such an impact on the lives of hundreds of young men. During his career Francis received several performance awards for his contributions to the smokejumper program. He retired in 1972 and passed away in 1998 at eighty-three years of age.

When a small group of the 1957 rookie crew got together in 2021, we reminisced about our years working for Francis and what a great leader he was. This prompted me to write about who Francis was and how he shaped our lives—truths we learned, what made Pappy the man we knew, and how the "Pappy experience" changed us.

In 1969 I was promoted to training foreman and grew under Lufkin's mentoring. In anticipation of his retirement, Francis followed through on his promise to provide opportunities and experiences to help me be more competitive when he decided to retire. He encouraged me to attend leadership and personnel management courses, involved me in regional and national smokejumper-related meetings and conferences, recommended me for instructing at regional training courses, guided me in getting my Master Parachute Rigger certificate, and more.

The 1970 Mega Fire Season

The 1970 fire season started off June 2nd when five of us Supervisory Smokejumpers flew to Cave Junction, Oregon, to help staff a rash of early-season lightning fires. We each made two to three fire jumps in two days before returning to NCSB to address lightning fires on the Okanogan. This fire season would prove to be a mega fire season for NCSB and a very busy one for our satellite base at La Grande, Oregon—several fire seasons compressed into one very intense, long fire season.

From June to mid-July, in addition to supervising the rookie training, I spotted jumpers on fires and jumped a couple fires myself. After intense lightning storms July 15, I split my time between spotting and assisting Francis as he fortified the base operation, which would soon grow from the typical forty NCSB jump personnel to 176, with jumpers boosting from all the bases in the country. This was the season's first "bust"—a spate of fire starts close together.

As Francis assumed the role of base liaison officer and safety officer, I became the primary jumper dispatcher and operations coordinator, assigning spotters, jump aircraft, and jumpers to fires scattered up the Washington Cascades, Olympics, and eastern Washington. We never had enough jumpers to fill our jumper requests. My regular work schedule started at 0400 when I reviewed the previous day's activities, reviewed and confirmed outstanding requests for jumpers, estimated when jumpers already committed to fires would return to NCSB, and finalized plans for the day. Lunch and dinner were usually brought to me in my office. Flight operations usually lasted until dark. At 2200 I clocked out. Before going home, I would often take a one-mile run on the runway.

The second major fire bust, resulting in hundreds of fires, started on August 23rd with subsequent storms over the next few weeks. Fires still raged through the third week of September.

Adding to the excitement of a record-setting year was the birth of our son Michael. On September 12th he was born in Brewster, Washington. Sandy was expected to be in the hospital for five days—enough time for me to go on a fire. After a hospital visit on the 13th, I jumped the Little Creek Fire on Lake Chelan. I was demobilized the following day, just in time to pick up Sandy and Mike. The fire season would go on for another six weeks.

By the end of the season the La Grande base recorded 65 fires and 220 jumps, while NCSB recorded a record 213 fires and 1066 jumps. Had there not been a shortage of jumpers nationwide, NCSB would have likely staffed dozens of additional fires, making an additional 500 to 600 fire jumps. The season ended with last fire jumped on November 2, 1970.

The mega fire season gave me the experience I needed to qualify me for the Base Manager position. For three months, Francis essentially turned the smokejumper operation over to me while he assumed a critical support role. I had more than 800 hours of overtime during the fire season, working seventy-five days with only a few half-days off.

The 1970 fire season experience was followed by several experiences and training to make me more competitive for the Base Manager position. Mentoring continued through 1972.

The Base Manager position would be advertised nationally, and several experienced jumpers from throughout the country were interested in the job. Francis—and Parachute Loft Foreman Dick Wildman—made sure I met the FAA Parachute Master Rigger requirements. I attended a leadership training course, was on the regional committee developing a smokejumper aircraft plan for the Pacific Northwest Region, and took a very active part in the National Smokejumper Manager's Workshop—and more. By late 1971 Francis felt that I was "competitive," and he made the decision to retire in the spring of 1972.

Just before his retirement, on behalf of the base supervisory staff, I presented Francis with a request for one last official act—that he would be our spotter for a jump on the hill just east of NCSB. He agreed and managed the mission as though he did this every day, when in fact he had not conducted a spotter mission since the early 1950s. The mission was flawless.

At 0905 on May 15, 1972, Francis signed off on the mission, the request noted as "completed."

In June, Forest Supervisor Gerhart Nelson informed me that I had been selected to succeed Francis B. Lufkin, a national pioneer legend smokejumper. I would become NCSB's second Base Manager. Indeed an honor, but with it a responsibility to uphold the Lufkin legacy. I felt the challenge and weight of my selection, but it was a dream come true! A new era in smokejumping had begun.

Challenges of a Rookie Base Manager

The NCSB staff in 1972 consisted of forty-five jump personnel, three pilots, three office staff, two cooks, a contract recon pilot, and a contract helicopter pilot.

Assisting me in this "rookie base manager" endeavor would be a group of very skilled and dedicated staff, committed to carrying on the Lufkin legacy. These included FAA Master Parachute Rigger Dick Wildman and Supervisory Smoke-jumpers Don Fitzjarrald, Mike Marcuson, and Jim Grant.

My goal then, and in the future, was to surround myself with competent and dedicated supervisory staff, smarter and more skilled than me—to manage the parachute loft chute packing and repair, to construct smokejumper-related equipment, to safely deploy jumpers in the most rugged country in the United States, to train both the new and experienced jumpers to be skilled mountain parachutists, to manage the para-cargo operation, to effectively supervise smokejumper and ground personnel on fires, and more. I inherited such good men from Francis. Now it was up to me to carry it on.

My first years as Base Manager were challenging and at times very difficult. Though I was mentored by Francis, he was a product of the Depression years and grew up with Federal agency fire and smokejumper values of the 1940s and '50s. The jumpers of the '60s and '70s were from a different culture, at times a culture that I had a hard time accepting. I felt that I was a bit of both cultures.

My challenge was to preserve the foundations and critical values of the early days—Lufkin's legacy—and to build upon the strengths and values of the new generation of jumpers.

The 1960s and '70s jumpers were more apt to challenge management decisions. Unlike Francis' era, when management

29

decisions related to employment policies, employee conduct, and hiring and firing were black-and-white and unchallenged, Personnel Management (Human Resources) more and more seemed to side with the jumper. At times I didn't know how much authority I had. Some of my decisions were challenged. A few "brave" jumpers weren't afraid to "counsel me" with their input—sometimes solicited, sometimes not. I listened, just as Francis listened to me when I had suggestions for changes in procedures and policy. Sometimes the counsel was a bit humbling but I, and the base, benefited from it.

One personnel issue that I had a difficult time with was beards and long hair. I was concerned about how our users, the fire managers, would view us. I probably overreacted, and it probably wasn't that big a deal.

Ten years later, on a three-week fire detail to Alaska, I grew a beard. After six months of the "facial hair experiment," I concluded that I wasn't a very good "beard person" and shaved it off, never to return.

My management style was to be an active, "hands-on" leader—going through the annual jump recertification and daily PT, as I expected all jump personnel to do. I wouldn't expect them to do something I wouldn't do. No double standard. I would go on the fire jump list and make periodic fire jumps and rescue/EMT jumps. Being an active jumper, I felt, would give me more credibility as their leader. I would be familiar with changes in jump equipment and chutes, jump procedures, aircraft used to deploy jumpers, and everything the jumpers were experiencing.

The Lufkin legacy was built on a firm foundation, pillars, which he established.

Lufkin's Legacy Pillars

1. Provide a dependable, high-quality professional firefighting service—smokejumper parachuting skills and aggressive firefighting
2. Adhere to smokejumper program policies and training standards
3. Train to a level that prepares the jumper to perform safely and effectively in the North Cascades—tough jump spots, marginal conditions
4. Develop and retain jumpers who can safely and effectively perform under changing and adverse conditions—using common sense
5. From the highly-qualified and experienced jumper crew, develop a work force with special services and skills—search and rescue, first aid/EMT, forestry support projects, etc.
6. Achieve a quick response—a seven-minute takeoff time after the alert

As the Base Manager I was often put in a difficult position of having to represent and support the policies and position of Washington, D.C., Fire and Aviation Management, the Pacific Northwest Regional fire managers, the Okanogan National Forest Supervisor and Fire Staff, the National Aerial Attack Specialist, and the NCSB jumper crew. I quickly learned that sometimes the values or policies of all of those were in conflict with the way I thought the program should be managed. I felt that the smokejumper programs and NCSB's future depended on how we were viewed by our users—the Forest Supervisors, District Rangers, and Fire Management Officers, and the regional and Washington, D.C., offices.

I also felt an obligation to do all I could to protect my jumpers and the jump program, sometimes having to make decisions unpopular with the crew or with regional management. This sometimes required the jumpers to accept unpopular management decisions, as well as decisions the Base Manager had no control over.

Maintaining NCSB's Relevance

The role of smokejumpers was being challenged in the 1960s and '70s. As helicopters were being more widely used, their capability significantly increased. Networks of helicopter landing spots and bases of operation exploded throughout the western United States.

In 1974, helicopter rappelling was introduced in the Pacific Northwest Region of the Forest Service. The Wenatchee National Forest was selected to pioneer the U.S. Forest Service program. NCSB, with our jump training apparatus, was selected to be their training center. The operational area would be in NCSB's historic operations area, the North Cascades of Washington. How I responded to this challenge is discussed below in "The Helicopter Rappel Challenge." The prediction was that rappelling was the new tool and smokejumping would be phased out in a few years.

As a new Base Manager, I certainly didn't want the Lufkin legacy to die on my watch. I felt obligated to do everything I could to keep NCSB and the smokejumper program relevant and provide a service that met the future needs of our constituents, the National Forests of Washington State and the U.S. Forest Service in general. I needed to develop a strategy.

That strategy was for NCSB to provide not only parachuting initial-attack firefighters, but also skills and services that would make NCSB a "go-to base" for special services and skills. We needed to provide jumpers with advanced Incident Management qualifications and jumpers who could manage wilderness fires using MIST (Minimum Impact Suppression Tactics). I needed to provide qualified Air Attacks to manage aerial activities over the fire incident, EMTs qualified for search and rescue, "C"-rated timber fallers (highest rating) for special timber falling assignments, qualified fireline explosive team members, aerial observers, helicopter rappellers, aircraft dispatchers, and personnel with other special qualifications. In other words, I would strive to make us "irreplaceable." Now the responsibility was on us to provide the training, experience, and services that would serve to protect our legacy.

Assisting the Local Ranger Districts

NCSB had traditionally supported the local Ranger Districts by providing jumpers for District projects, as long as they weren't needed for jumping. Jumpers "on loan" could quickly be recalled. A planeload of jumpers always remained at the base for a quick response. During the spring and fall prescribed fire season I volunteered our services. Not only were we providing excellent workers, our jumpers were learning a lot about fire behavior and crew management. Several jumpers went on to be Fire Management Officers.

Developing the Para-Rescue Capability

In spite of the Base Manager challenges, the 1970s were full of new experiences and professional challenges. In 1973 the local physician, Dr. William Henry, introduced Emergency Medical Technician training to the Methow Valley. Since I was in charge of first-aid training I elected to enroll in the program. The training and certification were certainly in the best interest of NCSB. I encouraged jumpers to do the same, as it would provide improved emergency medical aid to injured jumpers. Over the years we, in conjunction with Dr. Henry, developed a very effective para-rescue operation, serving both our smoke-jumper operation and the general recreating public. The full details about the NCSB's para-rescue program and how NCSB responded to two backcountry emergencies can be found in articles included in Part 2 of this volume.

Upgrading Smokejumper Qualifications

With years of firefighting experience, both on the ground and in the air, and by taking specific Fire and Aviation related courses in the interagency Incident Command System (ICS) curriculum, a jumper could become qualified for higher-level ground operation or aviation-related positions. The ICS curriculum is very similar to a university course of study: Start with the basic 100-, 200-, and 300-level courses; those in the higher levels of fire operations, i.e., top-level Incident Commanders and staff, take specific advanced 400- to 600-level courses. Each ICS position requires completion of a Task Book, or record of successfully executing the key elements of the position on an actual fire.

Through fire experience and completion of ICS courses, jumpers assumed higher-level fire positions on smokejumper fires or on large non-jumper incidents—Type 1, 2, or 3 Incident Management Teams.

In the 1980s I was a Type 3 Incident Commander and Type 1 Air Tactical Group Supervisor. I maintained my Type 1 ATGS rating after retirement, until 2016.

Air Attack: Another Responsibility

As a smokejumper spotter I had training and experience in fire strategies and tactics, fire aircraft capabilities and limitations, and intermediate-level fire behavior—and I was familiar with fire airspace communications and management policies.

In 1974, concurrent with my Base Manager position, I took on Air Attack responsibilities. Under the newly-adopted Incident Command System, the "Air Attack" title was officially changed to Air Tactical Group Supervisor, or ATGS. But in the fire world, the title Air Attack is still most commonly used.

The Air Attack works for the Incident Commander and the Operations Section Chief. On initial attacks, before the Incident Commander arrives on scene, the Air Attack initiates an initial strategy and set of support tactics while communicating with fire dispatchers and the assigned Incident Commander while en route to the incident.

The primary purpose of the Air Attack is to manage as many as fifteen to twenty aircraft assigned to the airspace (Fire Traffic Area, or FTA) over a fire incident. As aircraft arrive in the FTA, they are assigned an initial entry altitude and a position. Safe vertical and horizontal separation are maintained while the aircraft is in the FTA.

In addition to managing the airspace, the Air Attack advises the ground resources on strategy and tactics, monitors and advises on fire behavior and crew safety, establishes mission priorities, selects aircraft for specific missions based on their capabilities and limitations, directs water and retardant drops, and more.

During the course of the fire season, the Forest Service or regional fire dispatchers may assign the Air Attack to assume initial responsibilities over an emerging fire, to assess multiple fires in order to help dispatchers prioritize fires, or to join an Incident Management Team.

Upon retiring from my U.S. Forest Service career, I had been a a seasonal Air Attack for sixteen years. Assignments took me all over the United States and eventually led me to a another sixteen-year career with the 747 Supertanker program—and international aerial firefighting.

The Helicopter Rappel Challenge

The initial 1974 national program was headquartered on the Wenatchee National Forest, adjacent to the Okanogan National Forest. The NCSB smokejumper training tower was the perfect, and logical, place to do the rappel training. Once again, word on the street was that within a few years rappelling would phase out the jumper program.

My response to the "threat" was to work cooperatively with the Region and Wenatchee National Forest in helping them establish the rappel training and look for ways the two programs could complement one another. I did not want to project an adversarial response.

I proposed that NCSB EMT personnel, including myself, become qualified rappellers. This would certainly support an effective EMT para-rescue program. Each year NCSB EMTs renewed their rappel qualification. I made a couple of operational rappels to construct helicopter landing sites (helispots) near Lake Chelan. Two NCSB jumpers rappelled to a fire on the Okanogan. The rappel program experience served me well when I went to the USSR/Russia on the U.S.–Soviet Technical Exchange for smokejumping and helicopter rappelling. I maintained my rappel certification until I retired from the Forest Service in 1989.

"Other Duties as Assigned"

In addition to being the NCSB Base Manager I wore several other hats, including national and regional training course development and instructing, aircraft dispatching and fire-related projects assigned by the Okanogan National Forest Fire Staff Officer, and special projects for the National Fire and Aviation Management Director. From 1976 to 1989 "other duties" consumed about 50% of my time. The downside was that these duties resulted in a lot of travel and time away from home, fall through late spring, and a heavy reliance on my staff to manage the base in my absence.

I did feel, though, that expanding my involvement in regional and national fire programs would benefit NCSB.

National Aviation Course Development

I joined various course development teams to develop standard national-level courses for aviation, "S-270 Basic Air Operations" and "S-370 Intermediate Air Operations." These courses discussed basic- and intermediate-level wildland agency aviation operations—theories of flight, helicopter and fixed-wing capabilities and limitations, safety, tactical and logistical uses, aviation communications, landing area requirements, retardant drop safety, and more.

Firefighter Safety

In the early 1980s I was part of the development team for revising the Standard Fire Orders and Situations That Shout Watchout programs developed in 1957. In theory, by following the Orders and Watchout situations you would avoid life-threatening events. The revised course, "Standards for Survival," included a new version of the Standard Fire Orders and Situations That Shout Watchout, becoming the standard training course for all Federal wildland firefighters. Dale Longanecker, then the NCSB Paraloft Foreman, was featured in the Standards for Survival video.

Helicopter Landing Areas Instructor

As helicopters were being used more and more during the late 1950s and early 1960s for fire operations and for retrieving jumpers after extinguishing the fire, I had to learn the requirements for a safe landing area. From this experience I developed training materials and slide programs, which led to a three-week detail to develop more than twenty helicopter landing sites on the Wallowa-Whitman National Forest in the Wallowa Mountains of northeast Oregon and Hells Canyon. From there I became the regional expert in helicopter landing area construction and part of the Pacific Northwest air operations training team.

The Effects of Carbon Monoxide (CO) on Firefighter Safety

In the mid-1980s I was detailed to the Washington, D.C., office to review documents regarding the physiological effects of carbon monoxide on firefighter physical and mental performance, impairment possibly leading to firefighter fatalities. As smoke containing CO is inhaled, the CO displaces oxygen in the blood (hemoglobin). As the percentage of CO in the blood increases, the body's systems are negatively affected. It was suspected that the effects of carboxyhemoglobin on the heart, lungs, and brain reduced a firefighter's ability to respond to life-threatening situations.

My objective was to develop fire operation guidelines for fire managers. I reviewed previous Forest Service and other studies dealing with the topic. Questions I had to address included: Where in the fire environment are CO readings the highest and the lowest? What are the physiological effects of CO? What are the indicators of CO impairment? Could CO impair firefighter performance and contribute to fire fatalities? From this information I developed guidelines regarding what fire managers can do to reduce firefighter CO exposure, how to recognize impaired behavior, and how long it takes to recover from various levels of carboxyhemoglobin.

Minimum Impact Suppression Tactics (MIST)

During the mid-1970s I became interested in how modified fire suppression tactics could reduce environmental damage caused by current suppression tactics. Nationally, and locally, there was growing interest in how we should fight fire in the wilderness environment. With support of the Okanogan and Wenatchee National Forests and the Pacific Northwest Region, I developed MIST: Minimum-Impact Suppression Tactics. MIST outlined various suppression tactics that could be used to reduce, and in some cases totally eliminate, signs of human intervention: no traditional firelines, no cross-cut or chainsaw scars, no camp-related scars.

On some larger fires MIST could be used on certain parts of the fire while employing traditional tactics in other areas, such as where the fire butted against non-wilderness and other agency land.

FLIR: Forward Looking Infrared

In 1994 I was hired by the Wenatchee National Forest as their initial-attack Air Attack stationed at Pangborn Airport in East Wenatchee. My Cessna 210 aircraft was equipped with a Forward-Looking Infrared camera. In addition to routine air attack uses, the FLIR could see through thick smoke, illuminating the fire perimeter and hard-to-see spot fires. The FLIR would be used to evaluate a new fire retardant dropped from airtankers. Retardant was cooler than forest fuels and would show up on the FLIR monitor. From the imagery I could determine if the retardant was still effective or if the fire had burned through the retardant, allowing the fire to spread.

The FLIR was particularly valuable in locating the fireline perimeter during periods of heavy smoke and for guiding a crew to safety when the fire threatened their escape. From my FLIR experience, I wrote a FLIR training guide and conducted a national FLIR training course in Idaho.

Aviation-Related Dispatcher

Several times I was assigned to large-fire Expanded Dispatch as an aircraft dispatcher for mobilization and demobilization of fire resources. After evaluating the scope of the operation, the Incident Commander/Air Operations Branch Director's objectives, time frames, weather, and availability of aviation resources, my job was to select appropriate aircraft, and number of aircraft, for specific missions to support fire and other emergencies. From there I would set up flight plans for the missions. In setting up the flight plans I had to also factor in pilot duty regulations and the suitability of the airports/airstrips for the assigned aircraft.

One of the most challenging operations I had was the Mt. St. Helens Volcano Incident in 1980. For three weeks I was detailed to the Vancouver, Washington, headquarters for the Gifford-Pinchot National Forest. The assignment was large-scale and quite complex. St. Helens was very active, spewing ash almost continuously. The abrasive nature of ash was harmful to both piston and jet aircraft engines. On piston engines, ash could clog fuel filters and the oil system, while on jet engines ash particles could melt, solidify on, and damage the turbine blades, leading to engine surges, flameouts, and even failure. Ash clouds caused major visibility issues. The volcanic plume was subject to the prevailing winds. My flight plans had to be flexible, always having an alternative airport planned in case the ash threatened the primary airport. Ash clouds changed almost daily, affecting usable airports, safe flight routes, fuel logistics, and more. The assignment was challenging but enjoyable, like a big chess game—and rewarding when all of the pieces came together.

Smokejumper Aircraft Screening and Evaluation Board

In the mid-1970s I was selected to be a member of the Smokejumper Aircraft Screening and Evaluation Board (SASEB). The purpose of the board was to evaluate candidate aircraft for suitability to safely and efficiently perform the smokejumper mission.

Fire and Aviation Management, smokejumper managers, aircraft manufacturers, and board members could submit a candidate aircraft to the board for consideration. The board would review the aircraft's performance characteristics, potential suitability for the smokejumper mission, and compliance with established requirements. If the candidate aircraft passed "the paper test," it would be scheduled for actual cargo drops and personnel jumps. Based on the outcome of the evaluation, the candidate aircraft could be placed on the "approved" list and eligible for contracting. Not all aircraft made the approved list.

As a member of the SASEB I was part of the review team and an evaluation test jumper. Over the course of my career I jumped twenty-five different aircraft, several during SASEB evaluations.

The positions and experiences described in this chapter served NCSB and me well and led to many national and international opportunities as Base Manager—and after retirement from the U.S. Forest Service, many new opportunities.

National and International Opportunities

A Detail to the Washington, D.C., Office

After becoming NCSB Base Manager, I was selected for various national-level details in Washington, D.C., the National Interagency Fire Center in Boise, and the National Training Center in Marana, Arizona. In early November 1974 I was in D.C. to rewrite the smokejumper portion of the 5700 (Aviation) Forest Service Manual, Smokejumper Handbook, and National Smokejumper Training Guide. After the weekend I would do a D.C. morning TV show interview regarding the smokejumper program.

Meanwhile, what was there to do over the weekend?

Well, how about jumping a fire in the Appalachians?

The Sand Creek Fire, Jefferson National Forest, Kentucky

November 3, 1974. Here I was in Washington, D.C., a weekend off, and nothing to do—so why not join the smokejumpers in Virginia for a weekend of firefighting?

As it turned out, there was a lot of hunter and arson fire activity throughout the central Appalachian Mountain states (Region 8, USFS). In previous years a spring and fall smokejumper program, made up of jumpers from Region 6 (Washington and Oregon), had been established. The program had just been activated to fight the current fire situation. I volunteered my services since I had the weekend off, and I was only an hour from the action. On Saturday morning I flew to Virginia and to the base of operations at the Lonesome Pine Smokejumper Base in Wise, Virginia.

Without my fire gear, I had to go shopping in Wise. I bought a pair of work pants and a pair of cheap boots and got outfitted for a fire assignment.

On the following morning, November 3rd, a jumper request came in—a forty-acre fire on the Clinch Ranger District of the Jefferson National Forest. The fire was on the border of West Virginia and Kentucky.

It was windy. I believe we exited the Twin Otter over West Virginia, drifted over the power lines on the border, and landed in Kentucky. It was a leaf fire in a broadleaf forest, probably started by possum hunters, possibly by an arsonist.

After landing on the ground between a couple of leafless broadleaf trees, we began building fireline. The line was completed a few hours later, and we were released from the fire. Now I had to beat it back to D.C. and get prepared for my Monday-morning TV interview. A Forest Service plane picked me up at a local airport and flew me to Roanoke, Virginia, where I caught a commercial flight back to D.C. by 2200 hours.

On Monday morning I did the interview and resumed my D.C. Fire and Aviation detail.

Canadian Smokejumper Program: IFFS

During the 1974 fire season, the Yukon Lands and Forest Service planned to initiate an experimental smokejumper program. The program would be managed by a new consulting company, International Forest Fire Systems (IFFS), Ltd. of Vancouver, British Columbia. The principal of this company was Bob Henderson, an ex-NCSB smokejumper and professor of fire management at the University of British Columbia.

Since there was no active smokejumper program in Canada, the Yukon Lands and Forest Service made a request to the United States Forest Service for assistance in establishing the

Yukon smokejumper program. NCSB was specifically requested to be the base providing the training. The request was approved.

In April 1974 the U.S. Forest Service Director of Fire and Aviation Management, the Pacific Northwest Regional Forester, and the Okanogan National Forest Supervisor signed the agreement. On April 24, training commenced at NCSB. Supervisory personnel conducted the training of seven IFFS jumpers. NCSB/USFS provided and officially transferred all the required jump-related gear, including parachutes, to IFFS. A U.S. Forest Service Beech 18 jump plane was provided for the training jumps. The Canadian jumper training was intense and culminated with each jumper making seven training jumps.

Now to introduce the program to fire officials in Whitehorse, Yukon Territory. In May, Okanogan National Forest Fire Staff Officer Phil Cloward, Supervisory Smokejumper Don Fitzjarrald, IFFS President/jumper Bob Henderson, and I flew the Beech 18 to Whitehorse. The plane was piloted by NCSB pilot Dave Russell. There we participated in a fire conference and introduced the smokejumper program to Yukon Territory Forest Service personnel. Don and Bill made a couple of demonstration jumps.

In 1975 IFFS/Yukon Territory once again requested training assistance from NCSB, this time to train eighteen IFFS jumpers. The request was granted.

In 1976 IFFS expanded their jump program and used NCSB facilities to conduct their training, using IFFS personnel as instructors.

NCSB played a big part in assisting IFFS in establishing their program—training and the transfer of parachutes and an assortment of jump-related gear. What began in 1974 would be the foundation of the British Columbia smokejumper program, as well as today's reciprocal international smokejumper operations.

The U.S.-Soviet Technical Exchange Program

The Russian smokejumper program started in the mid-1930s with military personnel parachuting to fires located near villages in the relatively flat terrain of western Russia. After jumping near the village, the jumpers would organize the villagers into a work force to combat the fire.

After World War II their program expanded across their vast territory, which included the largest forested area in the world. By the 1970s the Soviet aerial program employed around 2,600 smokejumpers, most cross-trained to helicopter rappel. This was the largest smokejumper program in the world and was very progressive in their parachute development.

In the mid-1970s, the United States and the Soviet Union initiated the U.S.-Soviet Scientific-Technical Exchange Program. While on a high-level scientific forestry visit to the Soviet Union in 1974, the Chief of the U.S. Forest Service observed a Soviet parachute demonstration using the Russian Forester Steerable parachute. The Chief was quite impressed with the Soviet smokejumper program. At this time the U.S. smokejumper program was searching for a better-performing parachute to replace the FS-10 parachute. The Soviet Forester parachute might be just what the U.S. program needed. The Forest Service Chief committed to a smokejumper technical exchange in 1976. The exchange would include the smokejumper and helicopter rappel programs.

I was selected as the smokejumper and rappel technical expert, along with ex-McCall, Idaho, smokejumper Doug Bird, who at the time was a Fire Management Group Leader in the Washington Office. Doug would serve as the Chief of Party. The third member of our party was a Russian-speaking interpreter,

Alex Vasilivesky. Alex had grown up and lived in Poland during WWII. He immigrated to the U.S. after WWII, and he was employed by the Forest Service.

Our month-long assignment to the Soviet Union would be to review the Soviet smokejumper and rappel program—specifically to look at the Soviet "Forester" parachute.

After arriving in Moscow, we met with Nikolai Andreev, Director of the Civilian Central Air Base of the USSR (now Avialesookrana), and Russian Deputy of Operations and fire expert Eduard Davidenko to review our itinerary. Eduard would be our guide throughout the detail.

The itinerary included a visit to the Soviet fire equipment development center in Leningrad (now St. Petersburg) and to Petrozavodsk and the Karelien Republic, where we would observe a helicopter rappel, a fireline explosive demonstration, and a smokejumper demonstration. From there, we traveled to Irkutsk (at the south end of Lake Baikal) in Russian East Siberia to prepare for my jumps with my Russian counterparts.

While in Irkutsk, I completed a brief Russian smokejumper training course and shared "how we do it in the States." From Irkutsk we flew 400 miles north to Ust-Ilimsk Air Base, a small operations base located on the Angara River, where the jumps would take place.

While in Ust-Ilimsk, the objective was for me to make two jumps with the Russians from their 1930s vintage AN-2 bi-wing. I would make one jump with the American FS-10 system and gear and one jump with the Russian Forester freefall system, also using other Russian jump gear. Our objective was to return to the U.S. with the Forester chute. But the Russians had another plan—to use the Forester chute as their ticket to the U.S. the following year. The Soviet plan won.

In June 1977 Andreev joined me, Bird, and the NCSB crew at NCSB for a "reciprocal jump" and a formal presentation of the Forester parachute and jump gear to the U.S. Forest Service. Andreev was a certified Soviet smokejumper. Upon receiving the Forester parachute in 1977, we sent the chute to the Missoula smokejumper base and equipment development team to examine. The drogue stabilizing chute was sent to the Alaska BLM jump base. The Forester concepts were incorporated into the new Forest Service chute—the FS-12. The BLM incorporated the Forester drogue stabilizing chute into their Ram Air freefall system.

A detailed report on my two jumps in East Siberia is included in Part 2 of this volume: "Jumpin' with the Russkies in East Siberia."

The Jump That Made Me Shorter

Jokes have been made that repeated hard landings and compressions of the vertebrae would make you shorter. Well, it's true! I used to be an even six feet, but after a 1978 jump in the Glacier Peak Wilderness, I was 5 feet 10-and-a-half inches tall. A bad downdraft 200 feet above the ground and a "crash and burn" landing on a steep side slope slammed me into a rock. My right femur impacted a twelve-inch-diameter stone. The rock won! My femur was broken in multiple places.

A shot of Demerol eased the pain. A rapid medivac via the Chelan rappel helicopter took me first to see Doc Henry in Twisp, then on to Wenatchee's Deaconess Hospital. The injury required orthopedic surgery and seven units of blood. My leg was put in an open Bohler-Braun support splint and I was on my back for eleven weeks, half of that in Wenatchee and half in a hospital bed in my living room at home—all the time on bed pans.

After that first few weeks in Deaconess Hospital, I impatiently requested that Dr. Cadman release me to "home care." My impatience was countered by a threat to put me in a full-body cast. Sandy cried and pleaded with him to not do that. It was a "no brainer." Dr. Cadman won.

I stayed in Deaconess for five-and-a-half weeks, lots of time to evaluate my life and think about the future. I needed to reestablish my life priorities and where God and my family fit in to my "smokejumper life." I determined that I wanted to continue my career as an active jumper, leading the NCSB. Being an active fire jumper and spotter would keep me in touch with the troops.

While in Deaconess Hospital, I had a visit from a Wenatchee High School teacher and track coaching friend, Tom Black. Tom was also the lay minister of evangelism at the Wenatchee Free Methodist Church. On October 3, 1978, I recommitted my life to Christ and to family. I also asked God to grant me the physical ability to continue jumping for twelve more "accident-free" years, until age fifty, at which time I would retire. Note: He did, and I did.

The eleven-week "bed restriction" was followed by thirteen weeks on crutches. During my bed stay, the Forest Supervisor allowed me to work from home a few hours each day. Shortly after "graduating" to crutches, I agreed to a detail to the Washington, D.C., office. I was bored and wanted to get back in action. I loaded my travel gear in a red smokejumper equipment packout bag and headed for D.C. via Los Angeles, not an easy airport to negotiate.

After those thirteen weeks on crutches, I picked up running again, seven months from the day of my accident. I could run two miles, not pretty, not fast. The doctor would not approve me for jumping in 1979 but did allow me to helicopter rappel and to fight fire. During the rehab I discovered that the femur injury resulted in loss of about an inch and a half of bone length. Jumping would have to wait until 1980.

This was my only jump injury in 615 Forest Service jumps.

I returned to jump status in 1980, making another 231 jumps. Routinely I said a little prayer as I positioned myself in the jump door preparing to jump—and it worked: no more injuries. I never took even the most routine jump for granted. Every jump was serious business!

I jumped with a "short leg" for three years before making a very important life-changing decision: to have two short legs. Losing an inch and a half of (bone) height on just one side would likely result in future back, knee, ankle, and hip problems, right? I rationalized that evening up the leg lengths would help prevent these problems, and I was tired of adding lifts to my jump boots and other shoes in order to artificially even up my leg length. In 1982 I decided to shorten my "good leg."

Until I retired in late 1989, I remained an active jumper, jumping several fires each year when Base Manager duties permitted. I never had any leg or back problems.

More details are included in the article "Hard Landings Can Make You Shorter" in Part 2 of this volume.

NCSB Faces Closure

Predictions of Phase Out

With increased helicopter use and the introduction of helitack and helijumpers in the '50s and rappelling in the '70s, the question was (and continues to be), *What's the future of the smokejumper program?* Rumor had it that helitack would take over, and jumpers would be obsolete by the late '60s. With the introduction of rappelling in 1973, a similar prediction was made, and the jump program days were supposedly numbered.

The greatest threat to the NCSB legacy came in 1978 with a national smokejumper base study, initiated by the Washington office. The purpose of the study was to look at centralizing the smokejumper program, possibly eliminating some bases. Ironically, I was on the committee, the only smokejumper on it. A similar study was looking at consolidation of National Forests and Ranger Districts.

I favored maintaining the current decentralized national smokejumper program, thus maintaining NCSB as a permanent base. My input didn't carry much weight. Washington decided to centralize the existing smokejumper bases, eliminating the La Grande and Siskiyou bases in Oregon. NCSB was scheduled to become a "spike" (satellite) status under the Redmond Air Center in central Oregon. As a spike base, NCSB would be activated only when fire activity spiked and there was need for smokejumper services in the North Cascades/North Central Washington. NCSB would be staffed by Redmond jumpers only during the summer fire season.

Okanogan National Forest Supervisor Bill McLaughlin and I were determined to maintain NCSB as a permanent base. I also wanted to emphasize NCSB's historical significance—the birthplace of the U.S. smokejumper program. An historic sign commemorating this history was placed next to the administration building—hopefully to serve as an "NCSB anchor."

In spite of our efforts, and the support of local, state, and national politicians, the Pacific Northwest Region Fire Director proceeded—on paper—to reduce NCSB to satellite status in the future. While the dust was settling, NCSB would temporarily remain a small permanent base with eleven jumpers, counting me.

Stripped of Chutes and Sewing Machines

NCSB could no longer rig parachutes or manufacture jump-related equipment. All of the sewing machines were transferred to Redmond, except for a couple we "rat-holed." After chutes were jumped, they had to be sent to Redmond for repacking and repairs.

NCSB Staffing

With our jumper count reduced to eleven, the Region forbade the Okanogan National Forest and NCSB from hiring more jumpers. As I saw it, the plan was to "starve us out of existence." Our program couldn't survive with just eleven jumpers. I was offered a transfer to the Redmond Air Center as the Smoke-jumper Program Manager. With me out of the way, it would be easier for the Region to finalize their objective. But I declined the Redmond offer.

With strong support from Bill McLaughlin, we looked at ways we could increase our numbers, despite the Region's direction. Our plan was to hire part-time qualified ex-NCSB jumpers on a Call When Needed (CWN) basis. The jumpers, most living in the Methow or Okanogan Valleys, would go through the annual recertification training and would maintain current jump status. Two were ex-Supervisory Smokejumpers—John Button, employed by the Gifford-Pinchot National Forest, and

Ash Court, who was managing the family-owned Bear Creek Golf Course. The other three—Scott Duncan and Ray Henderson, employed by the Okanogan National Forest, and Mike Wright, employed by the Gifford-Pinchot National Forest—would be "on loan" to NCSB when needed for smokejumper duties. Ash Court would go on to be a CWN jumper for five years.

In 1982 four very qualified potential rookie candidates, Craig Brownlee, Patrick Baker, Gary Brown, and Chris Paul, contacted me expressing their desire to become NCSB smokejumpers—but they were unable to because of the Region's hiring restriction. As a way to get their foot in the door, they were willing to go through the training as volunteers. Once qualified, they would work as volunteers until they could be assigned to a fire, at which time they would go on the payroll. The Forest Supervisor and Fire Staff Officer approved the plan; the Regional Fire Managers were not pleased, but we prevailed.

The four volunteers were great jumpers and appreciated the opportunity. When NCSB regained permanent base status in 1984, three of the four were hired as regular jumpers. The fourth, Craig Brownlee, became an orthopedic surgeon in Wenatchee.

RAC Spike Base at Wenatchee

The Region set up a spike jumper operation out of Wenatchee, sixty-five air miles from NCSB. Jumper dispatches for fires in the North Cascades, even within sight of NCSB, were dispatched from Wenatchee. Okanogan Dispatch dispatched NCSB to some "Okanogan fires."

Saved from Extinction

During this dark period, Forest Supervisor Bill McLaughlin, along with Washington senators and representatives as well as state and local politicians, rallied on NCSB's behalf to maintain NCSB as a permanent base. Supported by a comprehensive 1984 Region 6 smokejumper program study, headed up by Ken Snell—ex-Missoula jumper, and then part of Region 6 Fire Management—the decision was made to maintain NCSB as a permanent base with twenty-one jumpers. Parachutes, along with "rigging privileges" and sewing machines, were returned to NCSB, and normal operations resumed.

I owe a special thanks and appreciation for those who hung in there during those dark years, 1980 to early 1984, and to the jumpers and outstanding supervisory staff of professionals— Dale Longanecker, John Button, Jamie Tackman, and Steve Reynaud—who then carried the program, and me, through the boom years of 1985-1989 through to my USFS retirement in 1989.

NCSB's Future

A 2015 base study appeared to support keeping NCSB as a permanent base with upgraded facilities and thirty jumpers. As of this writing, there has been no progress on upgrading the facilities.

Two Smokejumper Programs: U.S. Forest Service and BLM

In the early 1980s, the Bureau of Land Management (BLM) smokejumper program centered in Fairbanks, Alaska, initiated use of the Ram Air freefall parachute system. By the mid-1980s it became the BLM's standard parachute. The freefall system required exits from 3,000 feet, while exits from the Forest Service round-parachute static-line system were made at 1,200 to 1,500 feet above ground.

Operationally, the agencies worked together, which sometimes meant that both parachute systems might be in the same planeload, each exiting at their respective required jump altitude. Some fire managers thought that the Forest Service should consider converting to the Ram Air system, due to its greater forward speed and capability of jumping in higher wind conditions.

What did the Forest Service Base Managers think?

It was felt that the Forest Service should become familiar with the Ram Air system. In 1985, I, along with other Base Managers, went to Fairbanks and completed the BLM Ram Air chute training course. The BLM ground training was outstanding, culminating with seven training jumps. In 1986 we returned to Fairbanks for Phase 2 of the Ram Air training,

The Ram Air Conversion

Although we learned a lot about the Ram Air system and its advantages in high wind conditions, we were not ready to adopt the system for U.S. Forest Service operations. We felt that the Forest Service round parachute was safer and superior in the timber country of the Lower 48. I kept current on the Ram Air chute through 1989, making twenty Ram Air training jumps.

Since the beginning of the BLM Ram Air program, there have been four parachute-related deaths.

In the 2010s when the Forest Service Director of Fire and Aviation was considering converting the Forest Service round static-line system to the Ram Air freefall system, I expressed my concerns with regard to the safety of the Ram Air vs. the round system. I also had concerns about operational issues and the cost of the Ram Air system. In spite of my unsolicited input, by 2024 the U.S. Forest Service was totally converted to the Ram Air system, a widely-debated decision.

Retirement

Smokejumping, like structural firefighting and law enforcement, is considered a hazardous occupation. As such, a person who has twenty years of service and is age fifty is eligible for retirement. I met the requirements and decided it was time. I was also fulfilling "my deal with the Lord" to protect me from further injury—and in return I would quit jumping when I was of retirement age. He did, and I did.

As I prepared to turn in my jump suit and take my name off the jump list, I reflected on my career. I reminisced about how things changed from 1957, my rookie year, until I retired in 1989. I documented my memories of years past in an NSA article, "An Old Jumper Reminisces," in April 2025. The full article is included in Part 2 of this volume and summarized below.

I also looked back on my tenure as Base Manager, and what I learned.

Reminiscing

When old jumpers—actually, young ones, too—get together, the conversation quickly turns to their smokejumper experiences and jumps. With rare exceptions, jumpers claim that "the smokejumping days" were the best days of their life. That was certainly true for me.

During the past couple of years, I had the good fortune to get together with some close friends from the "good ole days," and as expected, the conversation quickly turned to our years together at NCSB, smokejumping—the tough jumps, the WWII rations we ate, the jump to a fire we were on, the beer we drank at Verla's Winthrop Café, and lots more. Two of those "old jumpers" have since passed away in 2024 and 2025—friends and memories lost.

These conversations prompted me to document many of my memories, the highlights of smokejumping from 1957 through 1989.

- Who the jumpers were—from college boys and ranch kids to "professional jumpers"
- Our boss, the legendary Francis B. Lufkin
- Our pay, and the $2,000 we made for a summer's work
- The tough four weeks of rookie training
- That first jump to a fire
- The gear we used and how it evolved
- The evolution of Forest Service chutes
- The evolution of smokejumper aircraft
- Lufkin's, and the Forest Service's, aggressive fire suppression policy
- The record 1970 fire season
- Major changes in the smokejumper program and the program's survival

I believe that my years of jumping were the "golden years" of smokejumping.

What I Learned About Being a Base Manager

- In January each year, meet with staff, including supervisory jumpers and admin personnel, to develop NCSB objectives for the coming year.
- Seek staff input on important issues or decisions—policy, personnel, promotion candidates, etc.
- Do AARs (After-Action Reviews) after periods of activity—be candid and critical regarding how the work can be improved; document and develop a plan or procedures for corrective action.
- Annually have staff evaluate my performance on key elements/criteria—likely the same elements your immediate supervisor will use when evaluating you.

- Have an "open door"—listen to everyone who would like to talk to you; listen to the troops.
- Don't compromise program safety or policies due to pressure from those "above you" who don't understand the consequences of what they are asking you to do.
- Maintain an active jumper role; keep your name on the jump list.
- Have high expectations of the crew, but don't expect them to be as committed to the program as you are.
- Be humble; learn from your failures and mistakes.
- Have your act together when you are trying to sell, or defend, the program.

Finally, in December 1989, I ended my smokejumper career. I had made 208 fire jumps, thirty-one EMT search-and-rescue jumps, and several forestry-related jumps. During my career I "bagged" eight or nine trees—a couple intentionally—but none over 130 feet.

As a member/chair of the Smokejumper Aircraft Screening and Evaluation Board, I participated in several "candidate smokejumper aircraft" evaluations, which included jumps.

During my career I jumped from twenty-five different aircraft, but the Ford Tri-Motor jumps for the documentary *Smokejumpers: Firefighters from the Sky* were two of the most memorable. Not only did I get to jump "the Ford" but I jumped attired in my mentor Francis Lufkin's 1939 red jump suit. What an honor! The Ford was flown by Penn Stohr, Jr., an ex-Johnson Flying Service DC-3 smokejumper pilot and friend.

Sole Proprietor and Consultant

Incident Air Ops

After retiring from the U.S. Forest Service and a couple-month vacation to Australia and New Zealand, I returned home ready to begin a new chapter in my life. That new life was to start my own business as a fire and aviation operations consultant and instructor. I would take advantage of my teaching credentials and the experience I gained during my smokejumper-Air Attack career.

In the spring of 1990 I started North Cascades Fire Service, a sole proprietorship. My clients were state fire agencies, the Bureau of Indian Affairs (BIA), and private firefighting companies. During the 1990s I instructed several Fire and Aviation-related courses for the Colville BIA/Tribe, the Yakama BIA/Tribe, Washington Department of Natural Resources (DNR), Minnesota DNR, and various private wildland fire companies. In the mid-'90s, I changed my company name to Incident Air Ops to reflect a more specialized interest in wildland Fire and Aviation-related consulting and instructing.

Interagency ATGS Guide

As mentioned above, in 1974 I became an ATGS (Air Attack Officer), concurrent with my Base Manager position. After retiring I continued my ATGS role as a part-time Air Attack, usually as a member of an Incident Management team or as an initial attack ATGS stationed at Wenatchee or other air attack bases in the West. I also developed various air tactical operations courses for state DNR and National Forest Service personnel.

Later in the mid-1990s I was contracted by the U.S. Forest Service to draft a national interagency aerial supervision guide—now referenced as the Interagency Aerial Supervision Guide. The handbook was designed to address the management of all aircraft assigned to a fire—tactical, logistical, and media. The following year I assisted the airtanker lead-plane pilots in developing a guide for U.S. Forest Service and Bureau of Land Management lead-plane pilots. Today the Interagency Aerial Supervision Guide covers all aerial supervision positions.

Firefighters from the Sky: The History of Smokejumping

During the 1990s, the National Smokejumper Association was formed to preserve the history of smokejumping—to be "the keepers of the flame." I was an NSA Director for several years.

As part of the effort "to keep the flame going," the board of directors decided to produce a documentary on the sixty years of smokejumper history. Emmy Award-winning television news and documentary producer Stevan M. Smith was selected to produce the documentary. I was selected to be the technical advisor.

Video interviews and historic research began in 1997. Air-to-air filming of live jumps from the Ford Tri-Motor were scheduled for June 1, 1998, departing from the McMinnville, Oregon, airport—home of one of the few remaining Ford Tri-Motor planes.

The cast was made up of a Ford Tri-Motor and ex-Johnson Flying Service Ford Tri-Motor pilot, Penn Stohr, Jr.; me, wearing Francis Lufkin's 1939 original jump suit; Steve Reynaud, ex-NCSB jumper, wearing 1940s vintage jump gear; and Steve Nemore and Eric Hipke, ex-NCSB jumpers working for the BLM out of Boise. Nemore and Hipke would jump BLM Ram Air parachutes. The jump master on the first jump was Mike Tupper. On the second sortie, Nemore would be the spotter and Tupper would jump.

The two-hour documentary would begin with a sunrise pre-takeoff jumper checkout of four jumpers: one attired in Francis Lufkin's red jump suit, one in 1940s gear, and two in 1990s BLM gear. After take-off, the action would be picked up over the Coast Range forests north of McMinnville. Photographer Steve Smith would fly alongside the Tri-Motor and film the exits. It all went well.

For me, the two Tri-Motor jumps were special. Although I started jumping in 1957, I had never jumped this historic classic aircraft. Now, after thirty-three fire seasons of jumping, I got my chance.

The Tri-Motor ended its smokejumping legacy in Idaho in 1967. In 1969, both the Ford and Travelair were completely phased out, to be slowly replaced by turbine-powered jump aircraft. To me, the Ford was symbolic of the smokejumper legacy; it was first used in 1940, flown by legendary mountain pilot Bob Johnson.

On June 1, 1998, I finally jumped the Ford Tri-Motor, a dream come true, and these would be my last two jumps—documented in *Smokejumpers: Firefighters from the Sky*.

A bit of drama preceded the jumps—acquiring U.S. Forest Service FS-12 parachutes for me and Reynaud to jump. The Forest Service refused to provide chutes. Remembering that the Forest Service, a few years earlier, transferred this type of chute to the jump program in British Columbia, I contacted the Canadians. The Canadians, remembering how they trained at NCSB in 1974 when they were establishing their program, strongly supported the documentary and supplied both the main and emergency chutes. The U.S. Forest Service was in a tizzy. How did Moody and Reynaud get those chutes?

As for Nemore, Hipke, and Tupper—apparently, they had not received official approval to participate in the Tri-Motor jumps.

As a result, they received a reprimand and disciplinary action, but with no regrets.

Training Firefighters in the Land of Genghis Khan

It was one of those "calls out of the blue" from my old Soviet technical exchange partner—Doug Bird. Doug, after retiring from the Forest Service, became an international consultant. One of his consulting jobs took him to Indonesia to develop an Integrated Fire Management program. The project was sponsored by the German Agency for Technical Cooperation.

Doug was then hired to help set up a similar program in Mongolia. The project needed a qualified fire instructor. Doug contacted me to see if I was interested. This sounded interesting and challenging. Why not? And my wife, Sandy, could share the adventure.

Devastating Fires in Mongolia

In 1996 and 1997 Mongolia suffered record fire losses—twenty-nine deaths, eighty-two people injured, thousands of livestock lost, and major losses of infrastructure, forests, and steppe. In 1996 Mongolia's loss was 26,000,000 acres—and in 1997, 31,000,000. By comparison, the United States average wildland fire acreage is about 7,000,000 acres.

There were heavy losses in the communities and area surrounding the Khan Khentti and Gorkhi Protected Areas. The fires were 100% person-caused. In 1998 the Mongolian government sought international assistance from the German Agency for Technical Cooperation. The objective: Develop an Integrated Fire Management Program for Mongolia, modeled somewhat after what the Germans had done for Indonesia under Doug Bird's leadership.

An interesting note: Up until the early 1990s, the Mongolians had an effective Air Patrol Service and 300-person smokejumper and rappel program modeled after the Soviet program. Some 90% of Mongolia's fires were detected and suppressed by the smokejumpers. With the collapse of the Soviet Union and loss of Soviet financial support, the Mongolian aerial program shrank to just a hundred jumpers, whose primary protection area was around Ulan Bator. (I do not know what the current status of the program is.) The slack was taken up by Civil Defense, which proved to be very ineffective. One of my students was the Civil Defense staffer in charge of fire suppression.

The Integrated Fire Management program would be headquartered in Mongolia's largest city, the capital city of Ulan Bator (UB). Jim Wingard, an American environmental lawyer, was in charge of the program. Jim and his associates were responsible for developing the legal documents establishing Mongolia's national protective areas. Jim concurred with Doug Bird's recommendation to hire me. Sandy and I prepared for the adventure.

After eighteen hours of air travel from the U.S. to Seoul, Korea, and another three-and-a-half hours on Mongolian Airlines to UB, we arrived. We reported to project headquarters where we would coordinate travel, get supplies for multiple weeks on the road, confirm our training objectives, and head for one of five fire-impacted villages. After a week of instructing, we would move to another village. The villages were north and northeast of UB. Most of our travel was on rutted dirt roads, occasionally forging rivers, passing through wildlands where Genghis Khan once roamed.

I was contracted to train five fifteen-person Mongolian Fire Management crews assigned to specific villages. The crews were made up primarily of volunteer workers, supervised by volunteer supervisors, although some received a small stipend. The fire training would be modeled after U.S. Forest Service basic firefighter training. The general terrain and forest fuels are quite similar: grass, pine, some fir, larch, and birch.

Instruction included Basic Fire Behavior (S-190), Basic Fire Suppression (S-130), Communications, and Incident Management System. The next phase of training would include Crew Boss Leadership and more complex fire strategy and tactics. The program equipped the trainees with fire gear and basic fire tools, Pulaskis, shovels, fire rakes, blowers, personal portable radios, even one chainsaw per crew. On two of the trips my son Mike, an EMT with firefighting experience, was my assistant fire instructor and taught a basic first-aid course.

While my track was fire suppression, Sandy's was basic fire prevention and education. Sandy, a certified teacher, along with a park ranger from England and a Mongolian Information Training Center Director, trained educators, community leaders, and rangers in basic fire prevention and education. 95% of Mongolia's fires are human-caused. The primary causes: campfires not fully extinguished, many during winter/early spring antler hunting when it's cold and windy; vehicle and chainsaw exhaust without spark arresters; and tracer bullets. The primary focus was on safe campfires.

We ended up doing six six-week assignments. We were there during every month, except December and January. The temperatures during our February detail were minus 20-30 degrees F. Using their outdoor toilets, without seating, was quite an experience!

Our team organized a national fire conference, constructed a Fire Management Headquarters, and produced several fire-related training manuals. The project equipped five crews with firefighting tools, one chainsaw, fire coveralls, and hardhats.

Sandy's team produced a fire prevention curriculum and training video, a ranger handbook, and a children's coloring book; created a fire prevention song; and introduced what would become Mongolia's "Smokey the Bear"—Sonorchon, the ever-vigilant white-chested squirrel, protector of the forest. The highlight for both the kids and rangers was making "some-mores," after which they were trained on how to properly extinguish a campfire.

While on his first detail, my son Mike met Soo Ing, a Community Fire Researcher and member of the Integrated Fire Management Team. Soo was doing an extensive research project on the causes behind three years of human-caused wildfires. She had been asked by Europe's leading wildfire expert, Dr. Johann Goldammer, to lead a study on behalf of Germany's international aid organization, the German Agency for International Cooperation. The project would eventually become her Master's thesis at the University of Freiburg, Germany. Her acquaintance with Mike would lead to Soo becoming our daughter-in-law, Soo Ing-Moody.

Seasonal ATGS Assignments Continue

After formally retiring as a career smokejumper and Air Attack (ATGS), I continued working for the U.S. Forest Service as a seasonal Air Attack—including both initial-attack assignments and large fire assignments as a member of an Incident Management Team on a large fire—a multi-fire "complex."

As an initial-attack ATGS through the years, I was assigned to several different air attack bases throughout the country. If the fire was not contained during the initial attack and the fire became large, an Incident Management Team would be called in, and its ATGS would assume Air Attack responsibilities. Initial-attack details took me to the Pacific Northwest states, California, Arizona, Oklahoma, Arkansas, Minnesota, and Texas. I served as the Wenatchee National Forest initial-attack ATGS from 1991 to 1994.

I also worked on several large fires as a member of a Type 2 Regional/Area Incident Management Team and several Type 1 National Incident Management Teams. I flew several hundred hours in helicopters and fixed-wing aircraft on assignments over large fires in Alaska, Washington, Oregon, Idaho, Montana, California, Arkansas, Oklahoma, Nebraska, North Carolina, and Tennessee. Later I would add Chile and Bolivia to the list.

Typically, on large fires the Air Attack works sixteen hours a day, every day, for two to three weeks, usually flying seven to eight hours a day. The workday starts at 0530 with an Operations Briefing, followed by an 0600 General Briefing. The workday generally ends after sunset, with an After Action Review of the day's operations.

My U.S. Forest Service Air Attack career spanned forty years, from 1974, when I began, until 2016, when I ended my seasonal Forest Service work. While on Supertanker assignments to Chile in 2017 and in Bolivia in 2019, I also flew Air Attack assignments.

My fixed-wing aircraft included everything from de Havilland Beavers, Mooney Mauls, and Cessna 182s to a PC-12, Commander 690s, and a G4 Gulfstream—even a DC-3 jump plane for an hour. Helicopter platforms included the Alouette 3, Hughes 500, Bell 206, Bell 407s, and an A Star.

Probably the most notable fire was the Rising Eagle Fire north of Twisp, in 2014. The fire started on Highway 20 across from the NCSB. Firefighting resources were heavily committed to battling the Carlton Complex Fire at the time. A fleet of helicopters was working out of NCSB. Conditions on August 1 were "red flag" for temperatures to reach over 100 F, moderate winds, and low humidity. I was assigned as an Air Attack on the Carlton Complex Fire.

Prior to being assigned to the initial attack on the Rising Eagle Fire I was working with ground firefighting resources located northeast of Pearrygin Lake. Instantly after the fire's ignition, the Air Operations Branch Director called me on the fire-net radio to report a new fire start along Highway 20, across from the smokejumper base—"spreading fast"—and directed me to head there and immediately assume Air Attack responsibilities.

I immediately "signed off" with the Carlton Complex ground contacts I was working with and headed for Rising Eagle. Knowing that there was a heavy helicopter with a water bucket located in the Okanogan Valley, I ordered it. As I approached NCSB I requested all of the S-64 Air Cranes and CH-47s, and a fleet of medium helicopters, to crank up and position at the south end of the airport. The helicopters were to maintain separation, dip/load water, and proceed to the south end of the fire, where I would intercept them with target directions. Their instructions were to drop on an assigned target, proceed north until clear of the drop area and smoke, return to the south end of the airport, and repeat drops; when dipping or picking up water, report on the radio that they (Helicopter XXX) were in the river dip site; after loading, depart, saying, "Helicopter XXX out of the dip"; after making a drop, say, "Helicopter XXX off the drop."

While the daisy-chain of helicopters got into rhythm, I had ordered a single-engine 750-gallon airtanker from Omak and the DC-10 out of Moses Lake as soon as available. The DC-10 had been committed to a fire in California but would join us on Rising Eagle as soon as it completed its mission. Super Scooper water bombers were also ordered and would work out of Pearrygin Lake. I also ordered two heavy retardant airtankers from Moses Lake and a relief Air Attack as I would need to refuel in Omak in a half hour or so.

I tried to prioritize helicopter drops but had to cease when the single-engine airtanker showed up. After he dropped his load I canceled another drop because I could gain more if I didn't have to clear the air space for the 750-gallon fixed-wing tanker drop. When the heavy airtankers and DC-10 arrived, the relief Air Attack would work out a safe separation of aircraft. Two airtankers from Canada were also ordered and assisted in the suppression.

After getting everything in motion, I was running low on fuel. After briefing my relief, I headed for Omak to refuel. From all reports the relief Air Attack conducted a very effective operation, stopping the fire at around 600 acres and with minimal structure loss.

The 747 Supertanker Adventure

During the fall of 2003 I received another one of those calls out of the blue—this time from Penn Stohr, Jr., now VP of Operations for Evergreen International Airlines.

Evergreen had decided to convert one of their 747s into an airtanker. Evergreen had the airplane but they didn't have pilots certified for low-level airtanker operations. They needed someone to train their pilots.

Why did Penn call me?

Through the years as a jump master, I had worked with Penn when he was a DC-3 smokejumper pilot. Penn also knew that, in addition to being a spotter, I was a certified Air Attack. Penn's call was to see if I might be interested in going to work for Evergreen as a consultant—and training the 747 pilots in tactical aerial fire operations.

After I expressed my interest in the position, Penn scheduled me for an interview with the President/CEO of Evergreen, Mr. Del Smith, and Chief Pilot Cliff Hale. The interview went well. I was officially hired and started work in Marana, Arizona, in early January 2004.

In early January I made a four-hour detailed presentation on airtanker operations to the entire Evergreen International management group. Soon we were off to Washington to meet with the U.S. Forest Service Director of Fire and Aviation.

To adequately train the 747 pilots for low-level retardant drop operations, I recommended that Evergreen hire ex-smoke-jumper, smokejumper plane pilot, and retired lead-plane pilot Nels Jensen. Nels and I would be the Evergreen aerial fire operations instructors. As the engineers developed the retardant drop system, Nels and I were developing a training curriculum.

From 2004 until its first drop on a fire in 2009, the 747 made hundreds of static drop tests and flight tests to develop the pressurized constant-flow drop system. A special drop course was set up at Marana to evaluate the effectiveness of the drop system from different heights above the ground. The FAA required several flights to satisfy their air-worthiness requirements, and the U.S. Forest Service required flights to certify both the aircraft and the airtanker pilots.

The 747 VLAT (Very Large Air Tanker) Designation

In 2004 the largest U.S. Forest Service airtankers were 3,000-gallon capacity DC-7s, C-130s, and P3s—all classified as "Larger Airtankers." The proposed 747 airtanker, with a capacity of 20,000+ gallons, and the DC-10 with a gallon capacity of 11,900, required a new classification—"Very Large Airtanker," or VLAT. The company name given to the 747 would eventually be "Supertanker," the largest airtanker in the world.

The 747 Supertanker drop system was a new concept—a pressurized constant-flow system consisting of ten integrated fluid tanks to hold the retardant or water, and eight air pressure tanks to expel the liquid.

Seated behind the Pilot in Command and First Officer is a Drop System Operator responsible for the retardant delivery system. The Drop System Operator programs the air pressure tanks and liquid tanks to produce the desired retardant coverage level, anywhere from 1 gallon per 100 sq. feet to 10 gallons per sq. foot.

The operational capacity of the Supertanker, after testing, was reduced to 19,200 gallons of water or retardant. The concentration of the retardant could be regulated, depending on what type of combustible fuel the Supertanker was dropping on. For light fuels the coverage level would normally be 2 gallons of retardant per 100 sq. feet. At this coverage level the drop system could lay a retardant line about two miles long. The heavier the fuel, the higher the concentration level. Heavy brush and logging slash required coverage level 8 (eight gallons of retardant per 100 sq. feet), producing a 0.6-mile-long line, 125-150 feet wide. The drop height above terrain or vegetation was 150-200 feet, later set at 200 feet. The loading time was about 25-30 minutes depending on airtanker base capability. The en-route speed above 10,000 feet was 575 mph to over 600 mph.

Preparing for Low-Level Tactical Operations

Concurrent with the drop tests and flight certification, my task was to train the Boeing 747 pilots in aerial firefighting strategies and tactics, and determine how to incorporate the world's largest retardant-dropping aircraft into standard airtanker operations. Never had there been an aircraft this large engaged in low-level retardant-drop operations.

My challenge now was to develop a training course to prepare the 747 "point to point" high-altitude cargo-hauling pilots for low-level tactical drop operations at 150-200 feet above ground/tree level. The course we developed closely matched the basic course for certifying Air Attacks and lead-plane pilots. The course was three-and-a-half days covering fire behavior, communications, capabilities and limitations of various aerial firefighting aircraft, strategy and tactics, fire area operational protocols, effective use of suppressants and retardants, lead-plane operations, and multiple fire operation scenarios.

In addition to this in-house Evergreen Aerial Firefighting course, the pilots attended the National Aerial Firefighting Academy, where they underwent twenty hours of aerial tactics training in the United Airlines 747 flight simulator, and three days of fire simulator training where they engaged in fighting three large fires of moderate to high complexity. The next phase of the training took place in the mountainous terrain north of Marana. Here the flight crews made low-level water drops in a variety of terrain scenarios.

European Marketing Tour

In 2009 we made a two-week marketing tour in France, Spain, and Germany. At each of the locations, we met with key wildland Fire and Aviation officials and made demonstration water drops to show our low-level drop capability. In central Spain there was an active wildfire. This was the Supertanker's first fire drop.

On the way back to the U.S., the Supertanker scheduled a refuel in Alaska. By coincidence, there was a large fire burning forty-five miles southwest of Fairbanks, the Rainbelt Fire. Evergreen offered a "gratis" drop to demonstrate the Supertanker's capability. The offer was accepted, and two drops were made.

During the summer of 2009, the U.S. Forest Service awarded Evergreen a Call When Needed contract. The 747 Supertanker made dops on two large fires in southern California—the Station Fire and the Oak Glen Fire.

INTERNATIONAL OPERATIONS

Israel, 2010: The Mt. Carmel Fire

In December 2010 the Supertanker responded to a critical fire situation in Israel, the 12,500-acre Mt. Carmel Fire near Haifa. The fire was caused by a 14-year-old boy smoking a water pipe. Tragically, the fire burned over a bus full of prison guards, prison staff, and prisoners trying to escape. The escape route was blocked by a fallen tree. A total of 44 lives were lost during the Mt. Carmel Fire.

By the time Evergreen cleared all of the U.S. political hurdles and we landed in Tel Aviv, much of the heavy fire activity was over. However, we did fly two sorties and dropped 38,000 gallons of retardant that was imported from France. Twenty-seven aircraft from thirteen different nations fought this fire.

Awaiting the Supertanker when we returned from our second sortie was Prime Minister Benjamin Netanyahu. After he spent time in the cockpit with our Chief Pilot, Cliff Hale, I had a several-minute "one on one" discussion with him about drop operations and retardant. He was very personable and asked very good questions. During his hour-long visit, I had two more encounters with him, and he always remembered my name. He was an impressive individual—sharp, personable, and well-informed.

A full article on the fire is included in Part 2 of this volume, "Israel's Mount Carmel Fire."

Mexico, April 2011: Northern Mexico Fire Complex

In April 2011 we were dispatched to Kelly Field outside San Antonio, Texas, adjacent to Lackland Air Force Base. We set up retardant operations for "across the border" Supertanker drops in northern Mexico. There were no suitable airports capable of servicing the Supertanker in northern Mexico. The fires were the result of a March lightning storm, which started multiple fires in the State of Coahuila, seventy miles south of the Texas border.

During the week, we flew twelve sorties, making twenty-one individual drops on multiple fires totaling 228,000 gallons of retardant. I served as the on-board Air Attack, advising the flight crew on where to drop and what coverage level to use. Many of the drops were to protect large ranches and valuable pasture and range land. Terrain ranged from rolling to very rugged. There was no organized ground support to follow up on our drops.

New Ownership: Global SuperTanker Services, LLC

In 2013, as the Supertanker drop system was being perfected and approved by the Forest Service, use of this new concept on U.S. fires was limited. At the same time, Evergreen was undergoing financial problems which would soon lead to Chapter 7 bankruptcy and the end of the Supertanker program under Evergreen's management.

In 2015, Alterna Capital Partners LLC, an investment group, purchased the Evergreen assets. The company was renamed Global SuperTanker. The new SuperTanker President, Jim Wheeler, took over the operation and rehired the Evergreen pilots, maintenance team, and me as VP of Fire Operations and Incident Response.

A significant improvement to the program was an aircraft upgrade, from a 100-series 747 to a 747-400 Freighter, more suitable for the airtanker mission. Along with improved aircraft performance, we also made improvements in the drop system—and the combined improvements required further coverage-level testing on the U.S. Forest Service test site at Fox Field in southern California.

With new owners and a Supertanker team in place, we initiated a major marketing campaign. Over the next couple of years, I gained thousands of "frequent flyer miles" as a member of the marketing team when we participated in Australian, European, Asian, and North American International Aerial Firefighting Conferences and trade shows. While in the host countries, we scheduled separate meetings with their wildfire protection agencies. At the European International Aerial Firefighting Conference in Nimes, France, I made a presentation titled "Just Another Tool: VLATS. How the 747 and DC-10 airtankers can be used to accomplish their aerial firefighting objectives." In North America our marketing zeroed in on the U.S. Forest Service, including meetings with the Undersecretary of Agriculture and staff, Director of Fire and Aviation, and state fire agencies in California, Oregon, Washington, and Colorado, as well as the British Columbia Forest Service.

We continued to make improvements to the drop system—but still obtained no lucrative U.S. Forest Service Exclusive Use long-term contract. Over the next couple of years we survived on short-term contracts with Israel, Chile, and Bolivia, and CWN contracts with Cal Fire.

Israel, November 2016

The 2016 detail to Israel was in response to several hundred "terrorist arson fires" plaguing the country. Once again, by the time we cleared all of the political hoops, we were behind the curve as far as fire activity. Forty-five aircraft from nine countries, including Russia, responded to the need. Most fires were relatively small. After a briefing at one of their military air bases, we were assigned an airspace to patrol and take action on fires in the assigned area. We responded to only three fires, one near Jerusalem.

Chile, January 2017

In late January 2017 the "perfect fire storm" hit Chile. Drought, low relative humidity, extreme temperatures, and high winds spawned more than a hundred wildfires, quickly over-whelming Chile's firefighting resources. Eleven people, including five firefighters, were killed. More would lose their lives in the following weeks. The fast-moving fires destroyed more than 900,000 acres of Monterey pine, eucalyptus forest, tree plantations, vineyards, and communities. More than 1,600 homes were lost.

After a complex "political discussion" between Global Super-Tanker Services, the Chilean government, and a private U.S.

company with direct ties to Chile, the Supertanker was dispatched to Santiago, Chile, an eleven-hour flight. We operated there for three weeks. Chile had no infrastructure for supervising or using and refilling large airtankers, and they were unfamiliar with the concept of lead-planes.

My first responsibility was to prepare and present a Supertanker Operations Plan briefing to Chile's fire officials, and to set up a format for the Morning Daily Operations Briefing—flight weather, fire update, fire priorities, safety issues, and assessment of fire operations. After assessing the fire situation, aviation operation protocols, aviation safety-related policies, and more, I conducted an operations briefing for the Supertanker flight crew and our lead-plane pilot. The plan called for me to, after the morning briefing, fly to the priority fire operation's area to assess fires and flight conditions. If flight conditions were favorable, I notified the command center and requested the Supertanker. A couple of days we flew as many as seven sorties.

We set up a water loading operation at the Arturo Merino Benitez International Airport in Santiago, Chile. The operation was serviced by the Santiago municipal fire department, "bomberos." The bomberos set up a system of portable water tanks filled by fire engines. From the water tanks the fire engines pumped water into the Supertanker drop tanks. They worked their tails off to load the Supertanker. After a few days our load times went from around an hour to eleven minutes, with an average of twenty-one minutes—not bad for 19,200 gallons. It was a great team operation. The bomberos did a super-professional job. Joining us on the tarmac was a Russian IL-76, a 10,000-gallon water dropper. Operations went very smoothly—a brotherhood of international aerial firefighters.

To help direct the Supertanker on low-level drops, we needed a lead-plane pilot and a lead-plane, a requirement for our U.S. operations. Jamie Tackman was added to our team. Jamie was an ex-NCSB smokejumper, smokejumper plane pilot, and U.S. Forest Service lead-plane pilot. After retirement he worked seasonally as a U.S. Forest Service lead-plane pilot.

The concept of lead-planes leading airtankers on drops was foreign to Chile. Due to the distance between the U.S. and Chile, and aircraft contracting issues, we could not provide a lead-plane, but we could provide a pilot. Chile would have to provide the lead-plane, but it had to be flown by Chilean military pilots. Chile provided a Chilean Army CASA 235 turbo prop and flight crew. Jamie, kneeling behind the non-English-speaking pilots, using hand signals and speaking over the engine noise with his limited Spanish, directed the pilots in lead procedures and maneuvers, not an easy task.

After one day the CASA 235 went in for maintenance and Jamie upgraded to a camouflage-colored Navy CASA 295, flown by English-speaking Chilean Navy pilots. Seated behind the pilots, and conversing in English and hand signals to avoid speaking over the flight crew, Jamie was able to very effectively direct lead operations. Jamie did a superb job and contributed greatly to the effectiveness of our operations.

My role varied. I served as a consultant, advising the Chilean fire officials on how to best use the Supertanker. Sometimes I served as a conventional Air Attack, coordinating resources over the fire and directing where drops should be made. Some days I would fly in the Chilean Air Force in a G4 "executive jet" to set fire priorities for Supertanker drops. Our mission call sign was "Raptor" and I was given the handle "Raptor." Our mission area for setting priorities was a 500-mile-long strip stretching from 100 miles north of Santiago to 400-plus miles south of Santiago, and spanning between the Pacific Ocean and the west slopes of the Andes Mountains. Our target priorities were protection of cities and villages, ranches/homes, key highways, infra-structure, tree plantations, and vineyards.

Our drops were often over, or near, villages and infrastructure. We were credited with saving villages and lives—and were a regular part of the daily news. During our time in Chile, we flew forty-six sorties, making seventy-six drops, for a total of 825,00 gallons of water dropped.

At the conclusion of our detail, the crew was recognized at a special Red Cross ceremony, during which the Supertanker team was awarded the Extraordinary Service Medal—the highest distinction awarded by the Chilean Red Cross.

UNITED STATES OPERATIONS

Upon return to the United States, we were looking for work for the 2017 summer fire season. As VP of Fire Operations and Incident Response, I monitored wildfire activity throughout the United States and advised Supertanker management where we might be able to get a Call When Needed contract.

Cal Fire (State of California) had been monitoring our performance in Chile. But it wasn't until the end of August 2017 that we finally got the call—a CWN contract with Cal Fire when numerous large fires broke out in northern California following a major wind event and downed power lines.

Our base of operations was the McClellan Air Tanker Base in California. On our first day we dropped on a couple of large fires, and the Cal Fire reviews were very good. Now we had to show how the Supertanker could serve as an integral member of the United States airtanker fleet. We needed to "carve out our niche"—a role for the VLAT.

When the fire season ended in December, we had flown fifty-one sorties and dropped over 900,000 gallons of retardant on multiple National Forests and the State of California—and hopefully ensured us of some work in 2018.

The Supertanker Mission and My Role

The Supertanker mission requires a lead-plane, or Lead, for conducting drops. The Lead may be dispatched with the Supertanker, or it may already be in place over the fire. Typically, the Lead is a twin-engine turbo prop suitable for low-level flight operations. The U.S. Forest Service uses the King Air 200 and 250, while Cal Fire uses OV-10s (Broncos). The Lead pilot is specifically trained and authorized for low-level missions, less than 500 feet above treetops/ground. Many of the pilots are ex-smokejumper plane pilots, highly experienced low-level cargo droppers.

Before (or sometimes after) the Supertanker arrives "on scene," the Air Attack, who supervises all aircraft assigned to the incident, communicates the Supertanker mission objective to the Lead; the Lead then communicates the mission objective to the Supertanker Pilot-in-Command (PIC). Before engaging in a retardant drop, the Lead makes a high-level reconnaissance of the mission area, followed by a low-level recon, checking for turbulence and hazards to low-level flight, and then flying the "emergency exit" route to locate potential hazards. The Lead then briefs the Supertanker pilot and instructs the Supertanker pilot of the drop objective, the retardant coverage level, the exit route after dropping, and exit altitude after making the drop.

Generally, a "show me" low-level pass is made to clearly identify the target. Next is a "live run," with the Supertanker following the lead-plane about 200-300 yards in trail. As they fly the drop route, the Lead describes the route, hazards to be aware of, critical altitudes to maintain, and, with a poof of smoke, identify where the drop begins and where the drop ends. Pilots are restricted to eight hours of flight per day.

The 747- 400 Supertanker requires a Captain, First Officer, and Drop System Operator for managing the ten retardant tanks and eight compressed air tanks. Initially, we had two Captains, two First Officers, and two Drop System Operators. In 2017 and 2018 we were training the two First Officers for a Captain's rating.

As Chief of Fire Operations my role with each mission was to evaluate the flight crew's performance and how it could improve. This was particularly important as we were also training the First Officers for PIC positions. I flew on about 125 sorties, experiencing 250 individual drops. I was in direct communications with the flight crew. Seated behind the PIC, I had a good visibility of the flight path and the drop objective. I monitored all radio communications between the command and dispatch, as well as between the Supertanker, Air Attack, and the Lead. At the end of the mission I conducted an AAR.

To give you an idea of what the AAR and my evaluation includes, let's go through the typical day at McClellan Air Tanker Base and a Supertanker mission, part by part.

What After-Action Reviews Cover

Arriving before the scheduled duty day, typically 0900, the Supertanker maintenance crew has checked over the plane and taken care of any of the previous day's mechanical issues. The flight crew performs an aircraft preflight inspection. Before the 0900 general briefing, or after the general Cal Fire briefing, the flight crew and I meet to discuss the previous day's operations and concerns. We all attend the Cal Fire daily briefing, which covers weather, general fire activity, expected fire activity for airtankers, accident reports, and safety issues/reminders.

Now it's wait for a Launch Order, or fire dispatch request. When it comes, it's a scramble to load the retardant, program the GPS and radio frequencies, and get FAA flight clearances. When we're ready to roll, we contact Dispatch for a radio check notifying them that we are ready to depart, taxi to the assigned runway, take off, and do a final radio call to Dispatch notifying them that we have communications, have lifted off, and are en route to the fire.

En route, there is a lot of communication with FAA air traffic control as we proceed from McClellan to the fire. When we are about fifty miles from the fire, we can pick up chatter on the assigned fire frequency between the Air Attack and Lead, and between the Lead and airtankers. By monitoring the communications, the pilot and I get a sense of what our mission will be. At about twenty-five miles from the fire, the Lead may direct the Supertanker to an IP, or initial entry point or place, where we receive further instructions regarding our mission and joining up with the Lead. Finally, the Lead instructs the Supertanker to meet at a specific location for the mission briefing.

During the mission I am observing and taking notes regarding different aspects of the action. I am particularly concerned about adherence to agency airtanker operations policy and protocols, communications protocols, how the crew interacts, personality issues, the effectiveness of the drop, how the Lead interacts with us, and the Lead's evaluation of the drop. If we are doing multiple missions during the day, I give a brief AAR on critical issues that need correction after each sortie. I do a more extensive AAR at the end of the day.

Another Season with Cal Fire

In 2018 we were again hired on a CWN contract and stationed at McClellan Airtanker Base in California. Because of our speed we also effectively served southwestern Oregon in the Medford area. Several drops were made on the large Carr Fire near Redding, California, and the infamous Paradise (Camp) Fire, where the town of Paradise was demolished along with a loss of eighty-five lives. We flew seventy sorties, dropping over 1.3 million gallons of retardant in California and southern Oregon.

My Fire Career Ends… "Kind Of"

In 2018 I was promoted to Chief of Operations and temporary CEO until a new SuperTanker CEO/President was selected. I gave notice that in June 2019, when I turned 80, I would retire.

I agreed that after the selection of a new CEO/President I would stay on to train the new CEO and my replacement, Chief of Fire Operations. Also, I would work part-time, as needed, during the 2019 season.

A new CEO/President was selected in late 2018. I helped to "vet" my replacement, Chief of Operations John Winder, a very capable retired Cal Fire career Fire and Aviation officer. I told John that I would be available to back him up, and I did.

2019 Bolivia Amazon Fires

In 2019 the Amazon forests from Brazil to Bolivia were threatened by drought and hundreds of land-clearing fires. The government of Bolivia did very little to curb the setting of forest-clearing fires. Under mounting political pressure and with an upcoming national election on the horizon, the government reversed its position, terminated the forest-burning program, and decided to take aggressive fire suppression action on existing and new fires. Many of the fires were in old-growth Amazon forests, some in the savanna, grass, and brushy areas. Wildfire operations were managed by the Bolivian military. Bolivia had very limited aerial resources and, like Chile, no experience with large airtankers.

In August 2019 the Supertanker was contracted by the Bolivian government for what was called "a widespread fire emergency" throughout Bolivia, much in the Bolivian Amazon Forest. After a few intense weeks of setting up the Bolivian operation out of Santa Cruz, Bolivia, John needed a break. In late August, I relieved him for two-and-a-half weeks. Within another week or so the Russian IL-76 water bomber would join the action, along with a large helicopter from British Columbia and one from the States.

Operating out of Viru Viru International Airport in Santa Cruz, our mission areas were north, east, and southeast of Santa Cruz. Our priorities were towns/villages, ranches, and infrastructure. Typically, after the morning briefing, I would fly to the day's mission priority and confirm if visibility was suitable for drop operations. If we had suitable visibility, I would notify dispatch and loiter until the Supertanker arrived. If we needed multiple drops, and if we had enough fuel, we would loiter until the Supertanker returned. If we were short on fuel, we would either return to Santa Cruz to refuel or go to the airport nearest the fire.

Generally, I flew eight to nine hours a day in a twin-engine King Air 350 lead-plane. I sat in the co-pilot's seat to the right of the pilot. My pilot was not trained in lead-plane operations and did not speak English. Some days I had an interpreter. Our mission was to intercept the Supertanker twenty miles from the fire. We would fly directly at the Supertanker, 1,000 feet below its altitude, make verbal and visual contact, and turn 180 degrees so as to be in the same direction of flight. At this point I would describe the drop location and confirm the vertical-separation flight route—how we, and they, would turn after the 747 drop. My aircraft would fly at 300-400 feet above ground level, the 747 at 200 feet on the drop. To communicate with my non-English-speaking pilot, I would use my limited Spanish vocabulary, hand signs, and crude drawings relating to what I wanted. After the drop, the 747 would accelerate and turn, usually to the left. The Lead would usually turn right to attain maximum separation or go straight ahead if we couldn't turn right.

When not flying in the lead-plane, I would fly in the Supertanker and advise the pilots. After a week I got two assistants to share my workload. I trained them on the "Bolivian operation." One of my assistants was an ex-Cal Fire Air Attack, Jim Gonzales, while the other, Matt Woosley, was an ex-NCSB jumper and current U.S. Forest Service seasonal Air Attack.

After John returned, I headed home. What an experience working with the Bolivian military and working fires in the Amazon Forest of Bolivia. The Supertanker contract lasted fifty-seven days.

Memorable Jumps

Numerous times I have been asked questions about my most memorable jumps: the most difficult, longest packout, toughest fire to fight, and so on. In this chapter I would like to make brief comments about several fires that, for various reasons, are memorable.

What makes a jump memorable? Well, perhaps the challenge of the jump—steep and rocky terrain, marginal wind and jump conditions, marginal daylight, a small landing area surrounded by tall trees, adverse fire behavior. Or, perhaps, on the positive side, the success of the firefight, experiencing an adventure in a pristine environment, jumping in a different state, maybe a landmark number of jumps. Overall, each was different.

During my thirty-three fire seasons employed as a smoke-jumper, plus the filming of the documentary *Firefighters from the Sky* in 1998, I made 615 jumps including 208 fire jumps, thirty-one search and rescue (SAR) jumps, numerous fire/forestry-related jumps, and a countless number of parachute and smokejumper aircraft evaluation jumps. Although most were "routine," some were more memorable for the various reasons mentioned above.

Earlier in this volume, I have already described my first jump to a fire—the **Squaw Creek Fire | Wallowa-Whitman National Forest | Imnaha-Snake Ranger District (Hells Canyon)** in 1957—and my 1964 jump with a major parachute malfunction, the Mae West over Jack Creek.

My comments on others which follow, some brief, some a bit lengthy, will tell you why each was memorable.

1958 | Andrews Creek Fire | Winthrop Ranger District | Okanogan National Forest.

About two hours before the fatal Eight Mile Ridge Fire smokejumper plane crash, and during a severe lightning storm, I jumped a small fire with squad leader Chet Putnam. The conditions were very marginal with recurring lightning and bad downdrafts. To reduce wind drift distance and turbulence, spotter Keith (Gus) Hendrickson dropped us at 800 feet above ground level, but we still encountered a bad downdraft. The downdraft "jetted" me downward, an estimated eight-second descent. The downdraft let up at treetop level.

Two hours after spotting us on this fire, Gus, along with three others, would die when his airplane crashed a few miles away on Eight Mile Ridge.

We quickly contained the fire and hiked to the road for pickup. We didn't learn about the plane crash until about 2300 hours, when we got to the Winthrop Café. The tragedy had, and still has, a life-long impact.

A fuller account of the Eight Mile Ridge crash can be found in Part 2 of this volume, "Tell Us About Our Father."

1958 | Little Chilliwack Fire | Glacier Ranger District | Mt. Baker National Forest on the Canadian border east of Mt. Baker.

We found remnants of a reserve parachute, apparently left by a member of the 555th Battalion black paratroopers who jumped to this location in 1945. We were twenty-four miles from a trailhead north of Marblemount, and we constructed a helicopter landing spot. Our very first helicopter ride, saving us a long packout with 105 lbs. of gear.

A full account of the 555th Battalion—the "Triple Nickles"—can be found in Part 2 of this volume, "Against All Odds." (The "Triple Nickle" uses the British spelling of "nickel.")

A summary follows.

My personal interest in the Triple Nickles goes back to 1957, when Francis Lufkin would tell stories about when a hundred Triple Nickles were deployed to NCSB to assist ten NCSB jumpers fighting the 180-acre Peavy Creek (Bunker Hill) Fire on the Canadian border.

I also learned that in 1945 Japan sent incendiary balloons across the Pacific to ignite forest and range fires in the United States—psychological warfare. To counter the attack, the United States launched Operation Fire Fly, enlisting 300 black paratroopers—the 555th Infantry—to help counter the threat.

Lufkin also recalled that twenty-two Triple Nickles jumped the Heather Creek (Parks) Fire in the Pasayten. Another fire was jumped out of Bellingham—the Chilliwack Meadows Fire along the Canadian border, northeast of Mt. Baker.

Fast forward to July 4, 1958, when I and three other NCSB jumpers were dispatched to the Little Chilliwack Fire very near where the 555th had jumped. As we were searching for a spot to construct a helicopter landing area, we came across remnants of a military reserve parachute. We concluded that it was left there by the 555th.

Fast forward again to 2020, when there was renewed interest in the 555th as they celebrated the 75th anniversary of their initial smokejumper training at Pendleton, Oregon, and their contribution to the 1945 firefighting effort. There were mixed reviews of their performance and their contribution to the 1945 firefighting efforts. I wanted to learn more.

As I researched the history of the Triple Nickles I tried to put myself in their jump boots: How well would I have performed?

I looked at the training they received, the chutes and protective gear they were issued, the experience of their jump masters in mountain-parachute operations, their jump protocols, tactical deployments, and practical mountain experience in steep terrain covered with tall trees.

My conclusion was: They were in an uphill battle, their training was inadequate, the chutes and jump gear were not suitable for the steep tree-covered terrain, and lack of smokejumper operations history greatly handicapped their operations. The 555th Triple Nickles performed admirably "Against All Odds."

The full-length article in Part 2 of this volume discusses all of this in detail.

1958 | Swamp Creek Fire | Mt. Baker National Forest | Skagit Ranger District.

On a ridge above Granite Creek, now along the North Cascades Highway, we ate WWII rations, had a thirty-mile hike (with assistance from pack stock) down to the Ruby Creek Guard Station, then moved by boat down Ross and Diablo Lakes to the tram at Reflector Bar—then drove to Bellingham and flew to NCSB.

1958 | Gilbert Peak Fire | Snoqualmie National Forest | Tieton Ranger District.

My jump partner, Leroy Gray, made a poor exit and got a leg tangled in the shroud lines. He descended upside down, all the way down, landing in a rock pile. Leroy cracked three vertebrae. The extent of his injuries was not known until after the jump plane left the area. We had very poor radio communications. We were able to get Leroy out the following day. Fantastic waterfall and alpine scenery.

1958 | Silesia Creek | Mt. Baker National Forest | Glacier Ranger District.

The fire, east of Mt. Baker, was a previous ground crew fire that was not fully extinguished. On a hot late August day, Leon Gale and I jumped, our cargo was dropped, and the plane flew away. Shortly after, the fire roared uphill and burned some of our gear. NCSB was out of jumpers, so Missoula sent over a DC-3 load of thirteen jumpers to help us out. Two days later we were helicoptered out and traveled by vehicle all the way back. The fire was about thirty-eight acres.

1958 | Barton Heights Fire | Wallowa-Whitman National Forest | Imnaha-Snake Ranger District.

On the west side of Hells Canyon, the fire was about one-half acre. It was the first time I saw borate retardant dropped. I got too close to the drop and was saturated in borate.

1958 | Reed Peak Rescue | Okanogan National Forest | Winthrop Ranger District (now Pasayten Wilderness).

My first para-rescue jump. My partner was Squad Leader Hal Weinmann. The victim was a hunter suffering from a diabetic emergency. We transported the victim by horse ten miles to the Andrews Creek Trailhead.

1959 | Goat Mountain Fire | Wallowa-Whitman National Forest | Bear Sleds Ranger District.

We were reinforcing a jumper crew already on the fire. On the exit, my jump partner, Doug Bernhard, positioned behind me, exited too fast, almost on my back. As we opened, Doug's parachute shroud lines almost immediately got entangled in my parachute back tray. Neither of us could manipulate our chutes until I released my back tray belt. This freed me from Doug, and we both encountered partially-inflated chutes for a few seconds as we were nearing the short timber below us and preparing to land.

1959 | Tunk Mountain Fire | Okanogan National Forest | Tonasket Ranger District.

A routine small fire, but we were dropped very low, about 400 feet above the ground. The spotter, after checking the wind drift, chose a different flight route—which failed to compensate for rising terrain below the exit point. We opened with only a couple of seconds remaining after jumping to get oriented and to maneuver our chutes to a safe landing spot.

1960 | Toketie Fire and Rescue | Wenatchee National Forest | Leavenworth Ranger District.

A 4th-of-July jump to a small, nasty fire in Toketie Creek, a small side-drainage off upper Snow Creek. In a very steep area, the small jump spot was surrounded by major rock outcrops, short subalpine timber, and a large rockslide. We took off from NCSB before sunrise, arriving over the fire about dawn. The wind was light, and Tony Percival and I were first to jump. We made it in to the steep, small spot, landing very hard. Next out were Gene and Gerry Jessup. Gene missed the spot by less than a hundred feet, broke out a treetop, and landed in the rockslide, dislocating several bones in his foot. The rescue pack was dropped, and we administered Demerol and prepared to transport Gene to Toketie Lake, a very difficult one-mile ascent.

Additional jumpers were dropped in a safer jump spot a mile above the original. By the end of the day, we had Gene to the lake and he was helicoptered out to Leavenworth, and then on to Deaconess Hospital in Wenatchee, where his dislocated toes were treated. We set up a gravity-sock waterhose lay from a nearby stream, and after two days we declared the fire "out." Over the two days on the fire, my work partner and I found more than fifty ticks on us, thanks to "periodic tick checks."

1960 | Patterson Ridge Fire | Umatilla National Forest | Pomeroy Ranger District.

A 300-plus-acre fire, the result of a major lightning storm over northeast Oregon the previous night. With a shortage of firefighters/smokejumpers, they could only staff our fire with six jumpers. Jack Wright broke his leg on landing, leaving us with five firefighters for a growing fire. I had to coordinate the medevac with a small Hiller 12E helicopter. While the DC-3 was dropping cargo to the two jumpers who jumped before we staffed our fire, we heard a "bang." We found out later that the tail wheel of the DC-3 struck the top of a fir tree. Fir needles were noticed in the tail wheel structure during the post-mission ground inspection.

1960 | Beaver Lake Fire | Okanogan National Forest | Conconully Ranger District (now Tonasket Ranger District).

After the release from the Patterson Ridge Fire, six of us were reassigned back to the Okanogan for a large, fast-spreading fire that started along Beaver Lake the day before. During the initial attack, a B-25 borate bomber from Wenatchee crashed while making a drop. Upon landing back at NCSB, seven of us, in two planeloads, loaded up and jumped the fire. It wasn't until I returned to the base that I learned that the pilot of the borate plane was my wife's uncle, George Carey.

1960 | Deer Creek Fire | Wallowa-Whitman National Forest | Chesnimnus Ranger District.

A 2,000-acre fire in steep and rocky terrain, mostly grass, in Hells Canyon. We jumped just before dark—my second fire jump that day. We fought the fire with gunny sacks, beating the grass-fire edge all night. By morning, when the "bums" from Burnside Avenue arrived by bus, the fire was contained.

1961 | Lizard Lake #1 and #2 | Willamette National Forest | Rigdon Ranger District.

We were repositioned to Cave Junction, Oregon, at the Siskiyou Smokejumper Base. Our dispatch was to the Willamette National Forest to jump two small fires in a dense stand of tall old-growth conifers. This was my fiftieth jump. After extinguishing the fires, we hiked ten miles to a pickup point.

1963 | Bunker Hill Lookout Project | Okanogan National Forest | Pasayten Ranger District.

The objective was to transport—using a mechanical "Tote Gote"—6.5 tons of building materials from where they were dropped to the Bunker Hill Lookout and assembled to make a ground-house. Upon completion of the hauling, we motored the Tote Gote to the Pasayten Airstrip. The trip was interrupted when we encountered 2,000 head of sheep on the trail a few miles north of the strip.

1963 | Mosquito Creek Fire (Petrified Forest) | Wallowa-Whitman National Forest | Unity Ranger District.

A late afternoon jump, very hot, down air, and a very hard landing. I numbed the bottom of my feet and popped my shoe laces.

1964 | Jack Creek Fire Chute Failure | Okanogan National Forest | Twisp Ranger District.

A full account of this parachute failure is provided in an earlier chapter. See page 19.

1965 | Kelly Lake Fire | Klamath National Forest | Happy Camp Ranger District.

Once again, we were dispatched to reinforce the Siskiyou Smokejumper Base at Cave Junction after a lightning storm. Our fire was a small one along Kelly Lake. The jump spot was a very small opening in large old-growth. I managed to maneuver between the monster trees, making it to the ground. The fire was a burning stump next to the lake, the packout only a mile and a half.

1966 | Sevenmile Creek Fire| Wenatchee National Forest | Chelan Ranger District.

The fire was up Railroad Creek, west of Lucerne and a few miles from Holden Village. The eighteen-acre fire was mostly slash from a recent logging operation. It was a very windy jump. We teamed up with the newly-formed Entiat hotshot crew, the Bushmen. It was very competitive line-building. Of course, there was no doubt in our minds that we won, hands down! After lining the fire, we were demobilized to Lucerne, where we managed to get a few brews before boarding the boat to Chelan.

1966 | Delancy Ridge Fire | Para-Rescue | Okanogan National Forest | Winthrop Ranger District.

I dropped Ben Hull and rookie Johnny Davis on the Delancy Ridge Fire in the afternoon. A few hours later, while they were working around the base of the fire, the top section of a large snag fell, directly striking Johnny. The impact drove his body into the embers. Upon notification of the accident, Lufkin dispatched me to provide first aid and coordinate Johnny's medevac.

The jump plane was prepared with medical gear, spotter Terry McCabe and four jumpers—John Gordon, Bruce McWhirter, Rich Pratt, and me—as the first-aiders.

We arrived over the fire about 1800 hours, just as it was starting to get dark. We were surrounded by an active lightning storm. The winds were erratic and gusty. Ben Hull, on the ground, relayed Johnny's latest stats and assessment: not good. The need for our medical assistance was grave. Ben's assessment: Johnny had internal injuries, a collapsed lung, broken ribs, an injured arm and shoulder, erratic breathing, and shock.

I decided to go ahead with the jump in spite of the lightning storm surrounding us. We decided to drop the medical supplies and medevac stretcher before we jumped, in order to know exactly where the cargo landed relative to Johnny's location. The stretcher was very bulky and required me and Gordon to assist McCabe to get it unjammed and out the door. The turbulent air made the cargo drop even more difficult.

Between lightning strikes we prepared for the jump. The wind, as indicated by the drift streamers, showed borderline jump conditions, gusty and variable. Upon exiting from the plane, we had a wild ride. Maneuvering into the wind, I drifted about a quarter-mile. My jump partner drifted at least a quarter mile further down Early Winters Creek before landing in the rocky terrain—but no injuries. I headed for Johnny to do another patient assessment while the other three gathered up the medical supplies and stretcher. The injuries, it turned out, were a collapsed lung, broken ribs, a broken shoulder, severe shock, and minor burns.

After administering first aid to Johnny's limp body, we carefully placed him in the stretcher and set out for the road—a pioneer road which in a few years would be the North Cascades Highway. After several hours we got Johnny to the road, loaded him into an ambulance, and drove an hour-plus to the Twisp Clinic for initial care. Johnny was then flown to Wenatchee, where he received extensive medical care. Johnny never fully recovered from his injuries and never jumped again.

1970 | Squadleader Fires | Rogue River National Forest and Medford BLM.

On June 2nd, southwestern Oregon and northern California had a rash of lightning fires. Only a few of Siskiyou's jumpers had requalified for the season. A contingent of NCSB Squad Leaders were sent to Cave Junction to assist. I jumped two fires on June 3rd, my birthday, and one on the 4th. Meanwhile a lightning storm hit the Okanogan and we were recalled to NCSB, the beginning of a record year for NCSB, which would end in early November.

1970 | Military Special Forces Training.

In June, NCSB hosted U.S. Army Special Forces for mountain-jump training. The objective was to train the military regarding use of smokejumper wind drift streamers to determine wind drift/velocity for spot jumping in mountainous terrain. We made two jumps out of the Special Forces C-119 aircraft. Exits were at about 140 mph, considerably faster than jumps from Forest Service aircraft—a noticeably much harder opening shock!

1970 | Thunder Creek #2 Fire | North Cascades National Park (previously Mt. Baker National Forest).

The fire was in very steep old-growth timber, south of Diablo Lake in Thunder Creek. The fire was several hundred acres. It had not been fully suppressed by a fire team and was abandoned after a quarter-inch of rain fell in late July, just a month before. The jump spot was a recently-constructed helispot surrounded by fallen timber. Ash Court and I were first out and landed in the helispot, after some skillful parachute maneuvering. Twenty-two of us jumped to this spot while another twenty-four jumped to a spot below us near Thunder Creek. We constructed new fireline where the fire had escaped, once again containing the fire. We then turned the fire over to ground personnel and were helicoptered to the Colonial Creek Campground along Highway 20.

1970 | Little Creek Fire | Wenatchee National Forest | Chelan Ranger District.

This was typical Chelan jump country—steep, rocky terrain on the south side of the lake. It was a mid-slope couple-acre fire. Thirteen of us jumped from the DC-3, including Siskiyou jumpers Mick Swift and Allen Owen, known as "Mouse," a four-foot-ten ex-Marine, the smallest man to ever be a smokejumper. We were supported by Wenatchee helicopter crews. It was a day after my son Mike was born. I was scheduled to bring wife Sandy and Mike home from the hospital in two days. I was released from the fire in time to pick them up.

1971 | Stub Creek Cabin Rescue | Okanogan National Forest | Winthrop Ranger District (Pasayten Wilderness).

While Winthrop Ranger District employee Jerry Sullivan was disposing of old blasting caps, he accidentally scraped a cap on a rock. It exploded and blew his hand off at the wrist and caused multiple skin injuries. Word got out to the Forest Dispatcher, who in turn dispatched the NCSB first-aid crew. We jumped just about dark, landing a couple hundred feet south of Stub Creek Cabin along the east side of First Hidden Lake. I treated the wounds and administered Demerol through the night. In the morning Jerry was helicoptered to the Twisp Clinic.

1971 | Copper Basin Plane Crash Body Removal | Okanogan National Forest | Winthrop Ranger District.

A private airplane flew low-level through Washington Pass, and instead of proceeding down Early Winters Creek, it turned into Copper Basin, stalled, and crashed about a half-mile south of the highway.

Okanogan Forest Dispatch ordered up the NCSB first-aid team. Eight of us jumped to the site of impact, a rockslide area. Upon examining the aircraft, I discovered two deceased men, badly injured. I reported my finding to the Okanogan County Sheriff. The Sheriff requested we extricate the bodies and move them to the highway a half-mile away, via helicopter sling. Not a pleasant mission!

1972 | Lufkin's Last Official Act | Spot the Overhead.

On May 15, 1972, I presented Francis with an "official request" that, as his last official act, he spot the Supervisory Smokejumper team from the Twin Beech jump plane on Cotner Hill, east of the base. He did, flawlessly, completing the request at 0905 on May 15, 1972.

1972 | Slate Creek | Mystery Fire.

My 200th jump, and my second fire jump of the day. A hunter fire.

1974 | Lake Laberge Road | Whitehorse | Yukon Territory Fire Conference.

After training International Forest Fire Systems, Ltd., Canadian smokejumpers, we were invited to the Yukon Territory to make a presentation at their spring fire conference. Invited were two NCSB jumpers—me (the Okanogan National Forest Fire Staff Officer) and Bob Henderson, ex-NCSB jumper and founder of the Canadian jumper company. We traveled to Whitehorse via a U.S. Forest Service Twin Beech jump plane and put on a smokejumper program presentation for the Yukon Territory Fire Management. We made two demonstration jumps.

A detailed account of the Canadian training was presented earlier in this volume. See page 43.

1974 | Lake of the Woods Rescue | Okanogan National Forest | Winthrop Ranger District.

In this EMT jump, I landed on the edge of frozen Lake of the Woods, north of Pistol Peaks. The patient had a perforated peptic ulcer, which, under Dr. Bill Henry's authorization, I treated with an I.V. and helicoptered the patient out to the Twisp Clinic.

1974 | Sand Creek Fire | Jefferson National Forest | Clinch Ranger District | Kentucky.

Full details of this jump are included earlier in this volume in the chapter, "National and International Opportunities." See page 43.

1975 | Buck Mountain | Winter Survival Training | DNR Loup Loup.

In February, as part of winter survival training, we jumped at Buck Mountain Lookout, landing in more than five feet of snow. We constructed a modified snow cave and igloo for overnight accommodations. The following morning we loaded our rescue sled with our jump gear and snowshoed to the Loup Loup highway.

1975 | Campbell Lake Water Jump | Washington DNR.

National smokejumper training required us to parachute into water/lake, as part of our emergency training in case we should ever accidentally land in a body of water. This jump was preceded by "pool training." All went well.

1975 | Dusty Creek Rescue | Mt. Baker | Snoqualmie National Forest | Darrington Ranger District.

While making a fire jump in the Glacier Peak Wilderness Area, jumper Pete Cutler landed in an old-growth tree, his chute collapsed, and he fell with a partially inflated chute, landing at the base of the tree. The fall broke his back. Ash Court and I were dispatched to head up the rescue response. Ash and I jumped into a dense patch of tall timber near Pete. My chute hung up in a tree, about forty feet off the ground. After administering first aid to Pete, we helicoptered him to a hospital in Everett, Washington.

1975 | Body Extraction | East Fork Prince Creek / South Navarre Peak | Wenatchee National Forest | Chelan Ranger District.

While descending a steep switchback trail, a horse rolled over its rider, causing fatal injuries. NCSB was called to locate the accident site and administer first aid. After several low passes, I located the dead gray horse, which blended in with the granite rock. EMT Michael Michael and I jumped. I landed near the dead horse and found the dethroned horseman on the trail above the horse. He was dead! We transported the body to a helicopter pickup point in the meadow below.

1976 | Crum Canyon Fire | Wenatchee National Forest | Entiat Ranger District.

Eight jumpers, including myself, were dispatched to a fifteen-acre fire between the power lines and Entiat River Road near Crum Canyon. The fire was spreading upriver, to the north, when we arrived. During the jumps, the wind system was switching from a south flow to a northwest flow—a cold front had arrived. The wind change carried us over the powerlines to a patch of scattered timber. As the wind shifted, so did the direction of fire spread. The fire spread was moving toward our landing jump spot, but we were able to save the gear—barely.

Immediately after the jumps, the spotter dropped our para-cargo in an estimated 40 mph wind. We quickly gathered our gear and cargo and hunkered down in a burned-out area until the fire front passed us. We then started firelining and burnout operations, which lasted all night. By morning the fire was 3,000 acres and had consumed our jump gear that was stacked in what we thought was a burned-out area. Eventually the fire was contained at 7,000 acres.

1976 | Soviet Tech. Jumps | East Siberia.

A full account of the two jumps I made as part of the US-USSR Technical Exchange can be found in Part 2 of this volume.

1977 | Bear Creek Soviet Technical Exchange Jump | Washington Department of Fish and Wildlife | South of Cougar Lake.

Twelve NCSB jumpers, Doug Bird, and Soviet Nikolai Andreev jumped at the Bear Creek training jump site. After the jump, Nikolai formally presented the Soviet chute and gear to Doug and me. Nikolai was the first Soviet smokejumper to jump in the United States.

1977 | Frosty Lake SAR | Okanogan National Forest | Winthrop Ranger District.

This was a major three-day search for one of Claude Miller's pack trip guests, apparently lost north of Frosty Lake. The weather was cold, windy, and wet. Twenty NCSB jumpers jumped near Claude's camp. The guest was found alive three days later, near the Canadian border, in relatively good condition. Ann Henry, Claude's head cook, provided excellent meals for the search crews.

1978 | Goat Peak Lookout Rescue | Okanogan National Forest | Winthrop Ranger District.

The lookout called in to report that she had been stung by a bee and was in anaphylactic shock. A quick response was critical. We suited up in a DC-3 as we were flying to Goat Peak Lookout. Jump conditions were good. I landed along the trail in the open saddle about 200 yards east of the lookout. I quickly ran/hiked to the lookout, where I administered a shot of epinephrine. Her symptoms had subsided, but she was still very anxious. She was transported to the Twisp Clinic for followup. In appreciation she made me a cake.

1978 | Broken Femur Jump | Wenatchee National Forest | Glacier Peak Wilderness | 4th of July Basin.

A full account of this jump can be found in Part 2 of this volume, "Hard Landings Can Make You Shorter."

1980 | Three Fools Pass Rescue | Okanogan National Forest | Winthrop Ranger District.

For the full story, see Part 2 of this volume, "Two Fools Jump into Three Fools Pass."

1980 | Sycan and Steamboat Mountain Fires | Fremont and Rogue River National Forests.

During the fall, a planeload of NCSB jumpers were dispatched to Klamath Falls, Oregon, to be on standby for possible hunter fires during the opening of the Oregon general hunting season. On opening day, I made my first fire jumps (two jumps) since breaking my femur—a bit tense, but all went well. I needed to regain my confidence, and I did.

1981 | Barnell Meadows CPR Rescue | Okanogan National Forest | Tonasket Ranger District.

This was an EMT jump with Kirk Hinkley. We were on a spotter training mission fairly close to Barnell Meadows when the call for EMT assistance was received. For this mission I was not in my jump gear. We were alerted of a possible heart attack victim, coincidentally located very near us. Since we had EMTs on board, we were requested to take action. I borrowed jump gear from another jumper on the plane and quickly suited up. A few minutes later we expedited the jump procedures and jumped near the victim. We quickly initiated CPR, continuing until the ambulance crew arrived. Although the victim was alive when we turned the patient over to the ambulance crew, the patient died en route to the hospital.

1982 | Silver Star Body Retrieval | Okanogan National Forest | Winthrop Ranger District.

The hiker/camper had disappeared in 1977 while camping near Silver Star Glacier. After several unsuccessful searches in 1977, searches were discontinued. It was presumed that the hiker had fallen into a deep crevasse and his body was not retrievable, too dangerous to recover. In 1982 a body was discovered at the terminus of Silver Star Glacier. The Okanogan County Sheriff requested NCSB to recover the body and deliver it on the North Cascades Highway to the Sheriff Department. Due to active snow showers in the area where the body was located, our jump spot would have to be halfway between the highway and the reported location of the body, the terminus of the glacier. We jumped and proceeded to the body location.

The body was presumably that of "Michael," the subject of the 1977 search. He was still in hiking shorts, wearing a light day pack and hiking boots. His body was "freeze dried" and weighed about 65 lbs., or less than half his reported "normal" body weight. Michael was folded into my packout bag and we proceeded to the highway. Jerry Alban spelled me off halfway down. We arrived at the drop-off point a couple of hours later and completed the transfer. The deceased was a missing orchard worker from the Methow area.

1982 | Lost River | #148 Fire | Okanogan National Forest | Winthrop Ranger District.

From the road the fire was about one mile up Lost River, burning along the river. Only two other jumpers and I were available. The jump spot was a gravel bar on Lost River, at the base of the fire. Jump conditions were windy, blowing up Lost River, about a quarter-mile of drift. We landed on the gravel bar and commenced to fight fire. All went well, and the fire was contained in a couple of hours with support from the Ranger District.

1983 | Fire #8864 | Alaska BLM | Ft. Yukon District.

In 1983 the interior of Alaska had a major fire bust. NCSB's entire crew was sent to Fairbanks to assist. Shortly after arriving at Fairbanks, we were dispatched to a large fire fifty miles north of Ft. Yukon. At the time I still had a metal rod in my leg from a femur shortening procedure the year before. I jumped five fires during the three-week detail. Later that year I had the rod removed. It appears on a wall plaque along with my "original rod" removed from my right leg in 1980.

1984 | Say Fire | British Columbia Forest Service | Merritt District.

The fire was burning in Canada near the Pasayten River, about a half-mile north of the U.S.-B.C. border, just north of the Okanogan National Forest's Pasayten Wilderness. However, the fire was on B.C.'s commercial timber land. The Forest Service feared that the fire would cross the U.S. border. The Okanogan National Forest put in a request to Washington for permission to drop U.S. smokejumpers in British Columbia to prevent the fire from spreading to the States. Washington approved the plan. By end of the day twenty NCSB jumpers were in Canada supporting the B.C. Forest Service.

I was in the first planeload, and my jump partner was Jerry Bushnell. The jump spot was a couple hundred yards just inside British Columbia, about a half-mile from the fire edge. The drift streamers indicated about 200 yards of drift—no problem.

Just as Jerry and I were about to exit, the fire "blew up," suddenly growing from around 300 acres to 600 acres. The blowup created a strong indraft wind. As we were descending, the indraft was strong enough to overcome our chute's forward speed, and we could not counter the drift toward the fire edge. The indraft drew us closer and closer toward the fire. Luckily, we were able to safely land a few feet from the fire edge in an area the fire had burned earlier.

We spent the next week assisting the Canadians. We were periodically resupplied from NCSB, but also enjoyed some great meals from the B.C. Fire Camp.

On our final night before demobilizing, the B.C. fire team helicoptered to our high mountain camp and delivered a wonderful chicken and steak dinner—plus some Canadian beer. That night it snowed on us. In the morning we hiked down the mountain out of the clouds, where Canadian helicopters were waiting to return us to the States. We sent a few American brews north to our Canadian friends on the return trips.

1985 | BLM Ram Air Training | Ft. Wainwright | Alaska.

In 1985 the U.S. Forest Service base managers were invited to go through the BLM Ram Air parachute training. Ram Air jumps were freefall jumps, instead of static-line parachute deployments. Jumps were made from 3,000 feet above ground. After several days of ground training, we made seven live jumps on the Ram Air chute system. The following year we returned to Fairbanks and went through their timber jump training. I continued annual Ram Air refresher training until retirement.

1985 | Cascade Creek Fire | Wenatchee National Forest | Chelan Ranger District | Chelan-Sawtooth Wilderness.

Also called the "Toilet Paper Fire." It was caused by campers who thought that in the wilderness you were supposed to burn your toilet paper. Fourteen of us spent four days working on this 450-acre fire. I was summoned to Federal Court in Spokane to testify regarding the fire but didn't have to. The fire starters were found "not guilty" because they followed "wilderness protocol" and burned their TP.

1985 | Bulldog Mountain Rescue | Colville National Forest | Republic Ranger District.

For a full account, see Part 2 of this volume, "Two Fools Jump Again."

1985 | Ink Lake Fire | Mt. Baker-Snoqualmie National Forest | Skykomish Ranger District.

Twelve of us jumped this four-acre fire in old-growth cedar. The jump spot was the shore of Ink Lake. The jump strategy was to descend over the lake and then land on the shore a few feet from the water in order to avoid the tall trees. We did!

1985 | Hubbard Creek Fire | Okanogan National Forest | Winthrop Ranger District.

I jumped the fire twice—once to do recon to help determine action the Forest Service would take, the second time to be the Type 3 Incident Commander leading jumpers and ground personnel on this several-hundred-acre wilderness fire.

We were to use minimum suppression tactics on the eastern side of the fire. The helicopter assigned to pick me up for a recon flight crashed on the North Fork of Wolf Creek minutes before it was scheduled to arrive. Pilot Joe Coke died in the crash.

1985 | Moody Fire | Mt. Hood National Forest | Estacada Ranger District | Bull of the Woods Wilderness.

This was my 500th Forest Service jump. The fire was a half-acre.

1987 | #43 Farewell Creek Fire | Okanogan National Forest | Winthrop Ranger District.

Very unstable atmospheric conditions created thermal updrafts. I was first out with partner Jay Moomaw. The usual ninety-second descent from 1,500 feet took twice as long. The next two jumpers took about seven minutes, and one of the last two about twenty minutes. He was in a thermal which took him north up the ridge about a quarter-mile or more without losing altitude. He then got in air that brought him back toward the fire jump spot, finally landing in the jump spot. The longest ride I ever witnessed.

1987 | Brush Creek #1172 Fire | Deschutes National Forest | Sisters Ranger District | Mt. Jefferson Wilderness Area.

This was part of a major multiple-fire episode extending from central Oregon to central California. All NCSB jumpers were dispatched to Oregon. Jay Moomaw and I made an initial attack on the Brahma Lake Fire, a small fire on the Deschutes National Forest, Sisters District, direct from NCSB. We quickly contained the fire and were relieved by a ground crew and driven to Redmond, arriving at 0200.

At 0500 we reported to the Redmond Smokejumper Base and prepared for another fire, along with three NCSB jumpers, Deed Fink, David Graves, and Matt Woosley, who arrived at Redmond the night before. Our assignment was in the Mt. Jefferson Wilderness, the Brush Creek Fire, a three-acre fire in old growth, growing fast. It was a windy jump.

After landing I ordered a planeload of reinforcements but they determined it was too windy for them to jump. A couple days later, our fire was over 300 acres and we were the 97th national priority. The five of us were the only firefighters on the fire. After a couple of days a ground crew would hike in, work a couple hours, and return to their home unit by the end of the day. After about six days our request for help was answered. On day nine we were released back to NCSB.

1987 | Scaffold Camp Creek | EMT Body Extraction | Okanogan National Forest | Twisp Ranger District.

A hunting accident was reported in the Scaffold Creek drainage, assistance requested. David Graves and I jumped close to where the accident was reported. After landing I located the accident scene. A deer hunter had been shot in the neck by another hunter. He was deceased. I requested an extraction litter, and it was delivered by helicopter. We carried the deceased to the road, where the Sheriff received the body.

1989 | Battalion Creek EMT Rescue | North Cascades National Park | Lake Chelan Recreation Area.

The Wenatchee rappellers and helicopter were working the Battalion Creek Fire. While lifting off the helispot, the helicopter crashed. Wenatchee Dispatch ordered NCSB EMTs to respond to the accident. Jamie Tackman and I landed next to the demolished helicopter, administered first aid to the pilot, and secured the accident scene. A second helicopter was brought in to transport the injured pilot. The pilot's helmet saved his life. The rotor blade had "whacked" him on the head.

1989 | Mission Peak Fire | Okanogan National Forest | Twisp Ranger District.

This was my 600th Forest Service jump, and my jump partner was NCSB jumper Casey Rose.

1989 | Reynolds Creek Fire | Okanogan National Forest | Twisp Ranger District.

This was my last fire jump before retiring, and Randy Vinson was my jump partner. The fire was a small hunter fire on the trail. The packout down Reynolds Creek Trail was seven miles.

1998 | Ford Tri-Motor Jumps | NSA Documentary | Oregon Coast Range.

Two jumps from the legendary Ford Tri-Motor wearing Francis Lufkin's 1939 red jump suit. The first jump is documented in the NSA documentary *Smokejumpers: Firefighters from the Sky*.

Defining Moments

Looking back on my fire career, there are a few defining moments—moments that at the time gave me great joy, or in some cases great sadness, fear, or wondering. Listed below are a few of those.

- Of course, that first training jump in 1957 and wondering if I made the right choice of a summer job.
- That first fire jump over Hells Canyon—this is reality, real fear, but to save face, I'll stick out the jump season.
- June 23, 1958, the day the jump plane crashed, killing three jumpers aboard—Keith Hendrickson, Gerald Helmer, and Bob Carlman—and pilot Bob Cavanaugh.
- Francis Lufkin firing me (and three others) for shooting grouse and pheasant out of season and without a hunting license—only to "reinstate" us an hour later following an "ass chewing," instruction to eat every bite of the birds, and never to do it again. A great lesson of grace.
- In May 1972 when Francis Lufkin spotted (dropped) me/us as his last "official act" before retiring.
- In 1972 being selected as North Cascades Smokejumper Base Manager to replace Francis Lufkin, and the reality of being "the man."
- In 1976 when I was selected to represent the U.S. smokejumper and helicopter rappel program for the U.S.-Soviet Technical Exchange Program.
- That first jump with the Russian smokejumpers in East Siberia in 1976.
- The jump with Nikolai Andreev, Soviet aerial firefighting chief, made near NCSB in 1977. Nikolai presented us with the Soviet Forester parachute,

which we basically copied, and in 1990 it became our standard smokejumper chute.

- When I broke my leg in 1978 on a jump in the Glacier Peak Wilderness—wondering if I would jump again, what effect it would have on my career as a smokejumper.
- Co-presenting the history of the smokejumper program with Francis at the Smithsonian Air-Space Museum in 1983.
- A couple of para-rescue jumps I made with John Button at "about dark."
- The Silver Star body retrieval mission, descending in my chute over Silver Star Creek, with snowflakes descending around me at the same rate.
- The day the Regional Fire Director announced that NCSB would become a satellite base under the Redmond, Oregon, base, that we could no longer pack parachutes at NCSB, and that all of our sewing machines would have to be transferred to the Redmond Base.
- The Regional Fire Director wanting me to transfer to the Redmond Base and take over their smoke-jumper program. No, thanks!
- In 1984, the day the Regional Office Fire Director announced that NCSB would remain a fully-operational permanent base and increased staffing to twenty-one jumpers, including me.
- In the mid-'80s when in the Regional Office in Portland, I was informed that I had been selected for a promotion to Regional Equipment Manager with responsibility for the region's smokejumper and rappel bases. I could still remain "jump qualified." I hadn't applied for the job, nor did I want the position. I turned it down.
- Regional Fire Director requesting my firing for my staff's refusal to use a jump plane that I/we felt was

unsafe and should be "decommissioned." My Forest Supervisor and Fire Staff Officer supported our decision, and the Director dropped the request. There were two instances when this model aircraft, in the drop configuration, lost control and lost several hundred feet of altitude before recovery. This model aircraft was later removed from the approved list.

- Making two jumps from the historic Ford Tri-Motor for the 60-year smokejumper documentary *Smokejumpers: Firefighters from the Sky*, eight years after I retired. The plane was piloted by Penn Stohr, Jr., ex-Johnson smokejumper pilot.
- Being selected to work with the 747 Supertanker team during the development years as air tactics instructor, marketing, later becoming Chief of Fire Operations.
- Recruited to be a multi-year fire training instructor of firefighters in Mongolia from 1998-2000.
- In 2019, after retiring, relieving the SuperTanker Chief of Operations in Bolivia, flying lead-plane in front of the 747 Supertanker at low-level for water drops over the Amazon forests.
- Being selected for the Walt Duran 2020 International Aerial Firefighting Safety Award.

The Final Retirement

At age 83, after thirty-three years of smokejumping, forty years of Air Attack, and seventeen years with the Supertanker program, accumulating a couple thousand hours in the air fighting fires, it was time to go through the "retirement ritual," again. It had been a career filled with adventure, challenges, and one heck of a lot of satisfaction. My greatest challenge and desire was to maintain, if not enhance, the Lufkin Legacy. I was also committed to help build a "Supertanker Legacy."

During my sixty-plus years in fire operations, I worked with a special breed of unique individuals:, smokejumpers parachuting in rugged timber-covered mountains; smokejumper pilots making tree-top cargo drops in canyon bottoms under turbulent conditions on a hot day; lead-planes leading in airtankers 150 feet above the tree tops under turbulent and smokey conditions and the airtanker pilot following the lead-plane through the turbulence and smoke; and the 747 Supertanker pilot maneuvering a 650,000 lb. Supertanker—jumpers and pilots with specialized skills, an adventurous spirit, and challenged by the environment they were in. Whether jumper or pilot, they shared a common gene.

While fire was certainly the central theme of my life, a theme initiated by a WWII paratrooper hero and a wild whim, at age sixteen, to go to Oregon and work in a sawmill for the summer, my life was more about the associations I had over sixty years of firefighting—family, friends, professional associates, and mentors. They were the people who believed in me, supported me, challenged me, and at times "called me up short." They encouraged me to engage in new and exciting challenges and adventures and provided me with opportunities that led to even more opportunities, some in foreign lands.

Now it has come to remembering those "good ole days," remembering your old buddies who you shared your life with, reflecting on the adventures, successes, and some failures. I highlighted some of those memories in an article I wrote for the National Smokejumper Association quarterly magazine— "An Old Jumper Reminisces," found in Part 2. Many of my old jumper buddies have passed, and the reunion numbers shrink.

Oh, to be a rookie smokejumper again!

Part 2
Stories

Tell Us About Our Father

Sixty-three years after their father's death, pilot Bob Cavanaugh's son Dennis reached out for information about his father's short time at NCSB, information that might help bring closure for Dennis and his siblings Denise and Kevin.

The following story is a response to that request. The story includes recollections of the "58 crew" who knew Bob and also information and excerpts from articles previously written by Jack McKay (NC-57), Doug Baird (NC-58), and Bill Eastman (NC-55) as well as Gene Jessup's (NC-57) book Friends I Have Found Along the Way.

This article was originally published in the National Smokejumper Association's quarterly magazine. Used by permission.

At approximately 1815 on June 23, 1958 Forest Service Twin Beech N164Z, piloted by Bob Cavanaugh, departed NCSB with a load of cargo for the Eight Mile Ridge Fire, Winthrop Ranger District, Okanogan National Forest, located 19 miles north of NCSB. Aboard were Senior Squadleader Keith (Gus) Hendrickson (NC-47), Squadleader Trainee Gerald Helmer (NC- 53), Bob Carlman (NC-57), a Forester, along to assess the multiple fires on the Winthrop District and to observe cargo drop operations.

At 1845, while circling for a second drop, N164Z crashed about .75 miles from the fire—all four aboard perished. Over the next few days regional newspapers carried the story and funerals were held. Unfortunately, however, the news sources, and the Okanogan National Forest, had very little information about pilot Robert Cavanaugh.

ROBERT (BOB) CAVANAUGH

Born on October 21, 1922 in Alameda, California, Robert Henry Cavanaugh went on to graduate from St. Elizabeth High School in 1940. Shortly after graduation he received an AA Degree in Criminology. In October 1942 Bob enlisted in the Navy flight program and entered into active duty in February 1943. In June 1944 he became a commissioned naval aviator and in 1945 was assigned to an anti-submarine warfare unit on escort aircraft carriers in the North Atlantic. After WW II Bob served in a reserve air anti-submarine unit stationed in Oakland. Later, while in inactive status, Bob furthered his education.

Bob was called back to active duty during the Korean conflict and was assigned to the carrier USS *Bataan*. Bob would later be sent to Pensacola to become a flight instructor for French and English military pilots. Bob married the love of his life, Dorothy, in 1952. In 1955 Bob's Naval career ended. He later flew for Mercy Flights out of Medford, Oregon and had logged considerable Twin Beech flight time. In 1957 Bob returned to Southern Oregon College of Education where he earned an elementary education degree in 1958, just two weeks before his death.

In the spring of 1958 Bob was hired for a US Forest Service smokejumper pilot position at the Okanogan Aerial Project (NCSB). Bob reported for duty in May 1958, and by May 30, he was dropping jumpers on their annual refresher jumps.

BOB BECOMES PART OF THE CREW

The 1958 season marked a couple of significant changes at the jump base—a new pilot and an aircraft upgrade—a US Forest Service Twin Beech replaced the old single engine Noorduyn Norseman.

The new pilot, as is the jumper's nature, had to be "assessed"— his personality, piloting ability, attention to safety, cargo drop accuracy, and pilot technique to facilitate a smooth exit with minimum opening shock (before the days of the D-bag.) In all of these areas Bob received very high reviews—this guy is going to fit in just fine!

Bob's "down to earth friendly personality" resonated with the crew. Gene Jessup (NC-57) recalls—"in the past there was not much interaction by pilots and the smokejumpers who rode in their aircraft... but Bob seemed to be just one of the jumpers. Most pilots were rather aloof but Bob was more like a big brother... he was well liked by everyone who had the privilege to spend time in his company."

On June 22nd, the day before the fatal crash, several of us, including Bob, a WW II carrier pilot, gathered in the bunkhouse to watch our favorite Sunday TV show—*Victory At Sea*, a documentary about WW II naval warfare in the Pacific and Atlantic Theaters.

The show featured carrier activities in the North Atlantic, Bob's old post. As the show progressed Bob added his first-hand account to the TV narration. He emerged as a real-life WW II hero, and further cemented his relationship with the crew.

Before "the D-bag days", jumpers were always bitching about poor position and hard openings which often resulted in bloodied clavicles, riser neck abrasions and, occasionally, a helmet ripped off. Some attributed it to the pilot—flying too fast, pulling too much power, inability to glide through the exit for an "optimum exit." Being sensitive to "our bitches" Bob fine-tuned the power settings, exit speed and technique to allow the jumper to attain good position resulting in minimal opening shock—it helped!

Jumper Doug Baird (NC-58) said of Cavanaugh, "Cavanaugh was greatly admired as a top-notch pilot... he was the best, someone we had learned to admire and trust."

THE FIRE SEASON BEGINS

The 1958 fire season was shaping up to be a busy fire season. The spring was unusually hot and dry with occasional thunderstorms. In early May the Snoqualmie National Forest had a 2,000-acre fire west of Snoqualmie Pass, the Bandera Fire—very unusual this early.

From Bob's arrival though mid-June the returning jumpers made their two required refresher jumps. The first fire of the season, a lightning sleeper, occurred on June 18th, on the Twisp Ranger District, Okanogan National Forest. This was Bob's first jumper fire and it went well—he was going to be a great jumper pilot!

Over the next few days temperatures climbed and T-storms were predicted to hit the area in a few days. On Monday, June 23rd the temperature would soar to 105 F. This was the sixth day of rookie ground training. After a few false alarms, around noon, two jumpers, Ron Roberts (NC-57) and Gene Gessup (NC-57) jumped the Rock Creek Fire on the east side of the Okanogan National Forest.

About 1400 two jumpers, Bill Eastman (NC-55) and Leroy Gray (NC-57), staffed the Eight Mile Ridge Fire, Winthrop Ranger District, 19 miles north of the jump base. The atmospheric conditions were very unstable with down draft conditions. The fire, in steep heavily timbered terrain, began to spread. At about 1530 two more jumpers, Jack McKay (NC-57) and Carl Dean Johnson (NC-57) reinforced the fire. About the time the reinforcements arrived the fire became very intense and was spreading quickly. The 20 rookie jumpers in training were dispatched via vehicles to support the four jumpers on the fire. When they arrived about 1800 the fire was estimated to be 3 acres.

Late afternoon two more fires were jumped on the Winthrop Ranger District just north of the Eight Mile Ridge Fire—two jumpers, Chet Putnam (NC-52) and Bill Moody (NC-57), on the Andrews Creek Fire. They witnessed bad downdrafts. The two other jumpers in the load, Jim Wescott (NC-57) and Roy Percival (NC-57), jumped the Disaster Creek Fire, the last fire Bob Cavanaugh would drop jumpers on.

TRAGEDY STRIKES

Returning to base N164 Z was refueled and a full load of cargo was loaded for the Eight Mile Ridge and Andrews Creek Fires. Keith (Gus) Hendrickson (NC-47) and Gerald Helmer (NC-53) would be the cargo kickers. Bob Carlman (NC-57), in the co-pilot seat would observe. The cargo consisted of hot meals, a Merry Digger (a several hundred pound mechanical fire line trencher), chainsaws, fuel and miscellaneous other equipment. At about 1745 N164Z departed on what would be its last mission.

Arriving at the Eight Mile Ridge Fire at about 1800 N164 Z circled to size-up the drop flight pattern then commenced with the first drop. Rookie Doug Baird (NC-58) wrote later "a perfect drop, placing it in a clearing near the fire base camp." The plane continued to the southwest, then turned northeast to set up for the second drop. Out of direct view from the jumpers they heard a "distant thud"—shortly after came the report from Sweetgrass Lookout that the plane had crashed. Elmer Neufeld (NC-45, CJ-44), Training Foreman, quickly organized a 10-person crew and hiked .75 miles to the crash site where they confirmed that all four aboard the ill-fated plane were dead—and then took action to contain the fire ignited by the crash. The specific cause of the crash was never determined but a T-storm in the area with severe downdrafts was probably a significant factor. The plane needed about 150-200 feet to clear the ridge.

As if to mourn the deaths, after midnight the lightning storms subsided, it rained for the next two days and the clouds hung low on the mountains—and the Okanogan Aerial Project was in deep mourning. We had lost four brothers.

During the next few days the overhead and crew discussed the tragic event and the risks inherent in smokejumper operations. What would the 20 rookies do, now only six days into their training? Surprisingly, no one resigned. A few of the experienced jumpers never fully recovered emotionally. The crash, in some way, had a permanent impact on all our lives— none more than the young family of Robert (Bob) Cavanaugh: wife Dorothy, sons Dennis, Joey, Kevin and daughter Denise. There were many questions left unanswered. Hopefully, this story, "Tell Us About Our Father," will help, in some small way, to bring a degree of closure.

REMEMBERING OUR LOST BROTHERS

In 2002 Tom Leuschen, Asst. Fire Management Officer, Twisp Ranger District, Okanogan National Forest, initiated a program to identify all the firefighters who lost their life while fighting fire on the Okanogan-Wenatchee National Forest. A bronze plaque would be placed at the site of their death. In 2003 Leuschen, John Button (NC-75) and Moody located the crash site. On September 26, 2003 NCSB jumpers placed a memorial bronze plaque and American flag on the site of the crash.

Although Bob's smokejumper pilot career was short-lived, he made a deep and lasting impression on the "58 crew." Six plus decades later our memories of him are still vivid—his friendly nature, "hero image" and desire to be a part of the team and "just a real nice guy," destined to be in the jumper pilot "hall of fame."

In August 2021 the 70,000-acre Cub Creek 2 Fire on the Methow Valley Ranger District burned over the Eight Mile drainage and ridge, and most likely the 1958 fire and the crash site. To be determined.

Remembering Francis B. "Pappy" Lufkin

In preparation for a group of 1957-59 NCSB rookie crew jumpers getting together, "Gino" Jessup (NCSB-57) commissioned me to write a piece about Francis Lufkin. The following is that piece, taken from my/our recollection of events and conversations, observations, published stories, official documents, letters addressed to Francis, school papers written by a family member, and speeches spoken at his memorials.

I had the added privilege of knowing Francis from 1957 until his death in 1998—as a jumper/supervisory jumper, as a "student" under his mentorship, and as a friend.

The following article appeared in the October 2022 National Smokejumper Association quarterly magazine. Used by permission.

Francis was a man for the times. He was a true pioneer of the smokejumper program, instrumental in establishing smokejumping in the early 1940s. Francis was highly respected by his jumpers, by the national jumper community, and by the US Forest Service. This was reflected by the many awards he received, a testimony to who he was. I hope you enjoy and can relive the "Pappy experience" and the best days of our life.

WHO HE WAS AND HOW HE SHAPED OUR LIVES

The seven of us [NCSB 57 rookies] have had the privilege of working for and being mentored by Francis Bourdette Lufkin, respectfully known to us as "Pappy." And what a privilege to have served under his leadership and to have been a part of the legacy he built at NCSB. Few people have had such a positive impact on the young men and women under his leadership—

123

350 jumpers until he retired, and another 200 plus, indirectly, after retirement through his enduring legacy.

In many cases Francis took a "calculated risk" when he hired us. Some of us were right out of high school or ex-paratroopers. Some were local farm boys. Some were wayward kids who needed direction and discipline. Francis gave us that opportunity to become men—if we were willing to follow his guidance. The "pappy experience" brought about a metamorphosis in many a boy on his road to manhood. Although it was not always apparent, the "Pappy experience" shaped our character by instilling life-long values—values which have guided us through life. But who was Pappy? How did he become the Pappy we knew?

WHO WAS PAPPY?

Francis was born August 1, 1914, in Auburn, Washington. At age 15 his father, during a drunken rage, ordered Francis and his brother out of the house—"they were old enough to fend for themselves." In the summer of 1929 Francis moved to Winthrop to live with his uncle, Ed Brengman, who lived up the Chewack (now Chewuch) at the Eight Mile Ranger Station.

In 1933 Francis graduated from Winthrop High School. Francis loved baseball and would walk to Winthrop on weekends to play a baseball game.

In 1933, Lola, his wife to be, moved to the valley and was working at the Palace Hotel in Winthrop when they met. In March 1937 Francis and Lola were married—a marriage lasting 61 years until Francis's death. From this marriage came twins Ron, and Raymond, then Larry and daughter Joyce. Ron and Larry both followed in the old man's footsteps becoming smokejumpers out of Cave Junction in the early 1960s. Daughter Joyce was a lookout for the Washington DNR.

A product of the Depression years of the 1920-30s and the 1940 war years, Francis worked at many jobs to support his family. He worked as a farmhand, a trail crewman, including being the crew cook, he built/maintained telephone line, cleared telephone right-of-way. He was a fire guard, a lookout (where he poached grouse), a logger in Oregon during the winter, a choker setter, a cougar bounty hunter, and a winter trapper in the Pasayten.

These exciting and demanding jobs equipped him to relate to, supervise and manage the post-war ex-paratroopers, CPS Conscientious Objectors, wayward boys, college party boys, city boys with minimal fire experience, and local farm boys. Along with these experiences, he learned firefighting skills, the "macho-man culture," a hard work ethic, supervisory/foreman skills, and acquired many of his favorite sayings and vocabulary we heard at break in the messhall, or when we were getting our ass chewed for a misdeed—like "you're spittin' in the wind," or "down the road kicking horse turds."

In 1939, Francis applied for and was selected to participate in the Parachute Experimental Project. He was selected primarily because he could climb trees. His role was to retrieve cargo and personnel parachutes, to set a smoke for the jumpers to see when making simulated fire jumps, to share his knowledge of the local area and his firefighting knowledge. On the last day of the project, one thing led to another, and Francis was dared to jump. The project leader said, "OK." They suited him up and took the famous picture of him in front of the Stinson. After less than 30 minutes of "basic training," Francis made one (first) jump. Lola was not in favor of him jumping—he confessed to her "after the fact."

In 1940 Francis was a member of the 1940 five-man jumper crew stationed at Winthrop Ranger Station. Other crew members included Glenn Smith, George Honey, and Virgil Derry. The fifth member of the crew, Dick Tuttle, was seriously injured in a pre-season climbing accident at the ranger station and could not continue jumping. On August 12, 1940, Francis and Glenn made the first fire jumps to Little Bridge Creek, west of NCSB—the first in Region 6, the Pacific Northwest Region. The first USFS jumps in the United States were made in Idaho on July 10, 1940, by Rufus Robinson and Earl Cooley.

Due to WWII from 1941-44, smokejumper operations were centered in Montana. Francis, a training instructor and rigger, would annually take the train to Montana for refresher training then return to the Methow to head up cargo drop operations and oversee jumper spike operations when a spike crew was brought in from Montana.

In 1945 NCSB was formally reestablished as a permanent base with Lufkin serving as aerial project officer managing a mix of ex-WWII paratroopers and CPS conscientious objectors. The base steadily grew with facilities constructed along the Methow River on the west side of the runway. As the facilities were being completed, along came the 1948 flood taking the facilities down the river. Not long before the Methow River took the new facilities down the river, Francis and Jim Allen (NCSB-46) loaded the gear into a truck and moved it across the runway. From 1948 to the early 1950s, the facilities were rebuilt on the east side of the airport.

In 1957 the rookie part of the bunkhouse was an open-end dorm, sometimes not tolerant of fellow rookie behavior. When an unofficial "lights out" edict was issued and not complied with, lights might be shot out.

In 1957, after a busy 1956 fire season, the crew was increased by eight jumpers. Roberts, Schwab, Gene Jessup, McKay, and Moody were members of the 1957 rookie expansion crew. In 1958 Steve (Dusty) Rhodes joined the Lufkin elites and Gerry Jessup joined the immortal group in 1959.

After 33 years leading the Okanogan Aerial Project/North Cascades Smokejumper Base, Francis retired in May 1972. Over his career he made 57 jumps.

As a final "official act," we presented Francis with a formal memo titled "End of Smokejumping Career—as your last official act, we the squadleaders and pilot, would consider it a privilege and honor to have you spot us on a training jump on Cotner Hill at 0815, May 15, 1972."

He agreed. Francis took us to 5,000 feet AGL (altitude above ground he made his first jump from) above Cotner Hill, and Pappy calmly and flawlessly spotted us as if he had been doing it continuously since 1940. A most special jump! Upon landing Francis signed the memo "Completed 0905 5-15-72 FBL."

During his career Francis earned several performance awards. Most noteworthy were the 1957 Department of Agriculture Award presented by the Secretary of Agriculture and in 1965 the Presidential Award presented by President Lyndon Johnson. The award was for economy—his ideas and inventions had saved the government several millions of dollars.

The awards highlighted his competence, excellent judgment, meritorious performance as an aerial project officer, commendable record in administration and operations, constantly seeking new and improved methods and better equipment, especially in mechanical equipment. He constantly looked for ways to make the jump program and firefighting more efficient and productive. In the mid-50s we experimented with a Tote Goat two-wheeler to speed up our return to the base, the Merry Packer for hauling out our jumper packs, the Merry Digger for mechanical fireline construction, and the Flail Line Trencher also for digging line.

PAPPY THE MAN AND TRUTHS WE LEARNED

How did his life experiences shape him, and indirectly us?

To many Francis was a quick-witted "mystery man", feared by some but respected by all. How did he always know what was going on in the loft when the doors were shut, or when someone was sacked out in the bunkhouse or loft chute bin during work hours, or out seeing Shirley the night before, or the bull cook "dancing with a broom" by the bridge, or hungry jumpers illegally shooting grouse on Cotner Hill after the mess hall closed, or driving brodies while under the influence, around the Noorduyn? Pappy always knew, and we paid for it.

WHAT DID WE LEARN ABOUT PAPPY?

Pappy was a man of faith, tough but fair. He was a man of few words, but when he spoke, he said a lot! He remembered his "earlier days" and showed us mercy for our "stupid acts." He had a great sense of humor, but not always apparent, and he deeply cared about his jumpers. When you demonstrated skill and responsibility, he rewarded you with more responsibility. After an ass chewing, the incident was over, and he didn't keep reminding you of it—it was a done deal. He was a man of integrity, he was prophetic, had a quick wit and great "one-liners."

We never had a doubt about his expectations. For the most part he hired (and fired) jumpers based on character and attitude and seldom was wrong. He had an uncanny ability to evaluate the situation when a jumper screwed up—"a bad bear" who could be rehabilitated. If not, he was shot or banned from camp.

He held you responsible for your actions, or lack of action. He always knew what was going on—both on and off the base. He spent hours searching US Government Excess Property for "good deals" that jumpers could convert into useful smokejumper related items, i.e., jump ropes, cargo chutes, cargo packing materials. He had a standing order with GSA for all kinds of surplus and GSA always gave him first crack at them. He loved lemon meringue pie.

HOW DID THE PAPPY EXPERIENCE CHANGE US?

The Pappy experience affected each of us in different ways. I believe the following are just a few:

- He helped us develop better judgment in situations that could easily go bad.
- We developed a stronger work ethic.
- We learned general values of life to guide us through life.
- We developed a strong and lasting sense of esprit de corps.
- Digging rocks on the airport helped develop our character.
- Pappy instilled a "can-do attitude" under sometimes very adverse conditions.
- It helped us to be more innovative under difficult situations.

INSIGHTS—WHAT A FEW OTHERS SAID

The following are just a few testimonies from family members and jumpers. Daughter Joyce: "In all my years knowing this man, I have never known him to make a decision that had not been carefully considered beforehand. His calmness in an emergency, his self-control in emotional situations is quite unbelievable."

Son Larry: Regarding drinking alcohol—"Dad was a drinker at one time, but he quit. He didn't preach about abstinence to others. He told a couple of young jumpers recovering from the previous night drunk 'you want to be careful with that stuff.' I never saw him turn anyone away who needed help. Several times he 'bent the rules' to hire a jumper who needed help in life."

Francis knew "there was a fine line between fear and respect." He had a keen sense of both, and he knew and used it to his advantage—when to give it to someone and when to be subtle. Keith Hendrickson (Gus to us) was very close to Francis. His death in the 1958 plane crash devastated Francis, as it also devastated all of us.

Jumper letter to Francis: A jumper looking for manhood after five seasons in the early 1960s, a letter he wrote to Francis after he had served as a medic in Vietnam. "...how much I have been taught by your example towards being a man... the way you handle the fellows and the many different situations that occur has spoken much to me. I have always appreciated your patience in allowing me to continue working after making so many foolish and short-sighted blunders."

SPECIAL PERSONAL PAPPY MOMENTS AND INSIGHTS

Each of us has a few special "pappy moments." Here are a couple of mine:

The 1959 grouse hunt (Moody, Bernhard, Satterfield, Zasada)—Caught red-handed by Francis, we were all fired on the spot and told to turn in our shotguns and jump pins. "Moody, report to the ad shack with these items." I collected the contraband, as directed, and reported to the ad shack and waited for Francis to complete his "cooldown walk" around the airport. Upon return he chewed my ass royally, returned the contraband, issued a very stern warning, and confessed to me about him (when a lookout) poaching grouse. That saved our asses!

1983—Six days with Francis in Wash D.C.—Smithsonian Smokejumper presentation—Francis told many stories about his many jobs. He could really get on a roll and start laughing. I brought up the 1959 grouse hunt incident, first time mentioned since 1959. We got a good laugh over it.

New Mexico Jumper Detail—In 1959 or 1960 I wanted to drop out of college spring quarter to go to Silver City on the spring jump detail. Francis told me bluntly that was a bad idea, would screw up my college graduation—think long term!

One-On-One—After becoming a squadleader for a few years, I could go in and talk to Francis about base policy. He would listen intently and approve or reject my input.

Running in jump boots—Convinced him running in jump boots can cause shin splints and we could be in our jump boots in seconds if there was a fire call. Policy changed.

Mentoring—I received much appreciated mentoring from Francis in the years leading up to my decision to go full-time under his mentorship in 1969 and after I became a full-time Training Foreman. He was very generous with his mentoring and the qualifying experiences I needed to qualify for the Aerial Project Officer position.

TIME TO GO

During Pappy's last few weeks, we had several talks. He expressed that he would find it difficult to continue, considering the many changes with personnel management, hiring and firing, ability to "manage" personnel, changing social culture, long hair, pot... "it's time to retire!"

In May 1972 Pappy retired and went to work for a retardant company returning to the valley each fall, followed by a winter vacation to the southern Oregon coast.

During the 1980s during fire busts, I hired Francis to manage the saw shack, cleaning, repairing, and sharpening chainsaws. He seemed to love it, telling stories to the jumpers and just being around the base. In 1981 the first female smokejumper in USFS/BLM history (Deanne Shulman from McCall Base) was detailed to NCSB during a fire bust. I got Francis and Deanne together to discuss their respective "pioneering history." It went on all day long.

OFF THE LIST

In 1998, at the age of 83, Pappy passed away. His name was ceremoniously removed from the Jump List. A memorial in his honor was held at NCSB May 2, 1998.

CLOSING

As I wind this up, I can only reminisce about our early jumper days, rookie training, our bonding experiences, life in the bunkhouse, Shirley Parties, the good jumps and the bad ones, the Eight Mile crash, times at Verla's Ponderosa Room, picking rocks, the "Bad Bear" incidents, and how through it all, Pappy put up with us. In the process we emerged a little bit closer to manhood and adult responsibility. Pappy greatly influenced our life, and he continues to do so today. His parting words: "Keep the sunny side up." Thanks Pappy!

Small Airport Handles GIANT Mobilization

The following article is a condensed version of an article Francis Lufkin and Bill Moody wrote for Fire Management Today *(U.S. Forest Service) following the 1970 fire season. It describes the impact the 1970 July fire busts had on NCSB—facilities, organization, and its individual air operations.*

This article covers only the July 1970 fire bust. In August it was a repeat, but with 186 jumpers and an impact similar to the July bust, which slowed in early August due to a quarter-inch rain. The rain quickly evaporated, and we were set up for "round two," which lasted from August 23 through much of September.

North Cascades Smokejumper Base, with its normal 36-man base with two jump aircraft, between July 16-31, 1970 became a major multi-function air service, fire cache supply, mobilization and demobilization center, operating around the clock. More than 350 people and over 50 aircraft were assigned to the total operation during the peak of the activity. The messhall provided over 800 meals a day, including hot meals dropped to firefighters on the fireline.

Smokejumper Force Grew

By the third day of the bust the smokejumper force at NCSB grew to 176 jumpers. Jumpers from every smokejumper unit in Regions 1,4, 5 and 6 participated. In the first 4 days July 16-19, 329 fire jumps were made. Between July 15 and 27, 496 jumps were made on 85 fires, with a record 103 jumps made on July 16. The smokejumper demand was so great NCSB was out of jumpers several times during the first eight days. A high percentage of the jumps were made in extremely rugged country under adverse wind and fire conditions. In spite of tremendous fatigue, only one serious and three minor injuries occurred.

3,000 Firefighters Arrived

Because NCSB was close to fires on the Okanogan National Forest NCSB became the logical mobilization-demobilization center for more than 3,000 firefighters. After arriving at Moses Lake on large jets the firefighter crews were shuttled to Omak, Washington and NCSB by a fleet of DC-3s and DC-4s. Most crews were fed and bedded down at NCSB while waiting to transfer to fires or later, waiting for demobilization aircraft. The messhall served 8,700 hot meals during one 10-day period.

Air Traffic Was Tight

For several days air traffic at NCSB exceeded that of Spokane International Airport. For a 10-day period NCSB averaged 325 take offs and landings. Between July 16 and 19, 1,150 take off and landings were made on NCSB's 5,000 ft. airport. All air traffic advisory communications were handled by the NCSB dispatcher using Okanogan Forest New Air Net of 122.8 frequency.

Visibility Issues

Thick smoke from numerous fires in the area hampered flight operations. Inbound flights from the south often followed the Methow River. Pilots claimed they were following IFR procedures, "I Fly River."

On the fifth day, a temporary FAA air traffic control station, operating out of the back of a pickup truck, was set up and operated 24 hours a day. This was done because, while the Forest Service could not authorize straight-in landings and take offs, the FAA controller could. The traffic control station made possible more take offs and landings and eliminated aircraft "stacking" overhead.

Total air traffic between July 16 and 31 was recorded at 3,700 take offs and landings, all without incident. Temporary field lights permitted 24-hour airport use. Aircraft assigned to the fires included six smokejumper para-cargo dropping aircraft, including DC-3, one DC-4 , multiple Twin Beech and one C-46 passenger-freight transport aircraft, five air attack lead planes, four aerial detection planes, and a fleet of small aircraft used for special missions and passenger haul. All fixed wing aerial retardant aircraft operated out of Wenatchee or Omak airports.

Helicopter Operations

At the peak of activity 23 helicopters, including six heavy turbines, were assigned to NCSB to form a helicopter pool. In the course of the bust the helicopters transported 10,201 passengers, and 459,037 lbs. of cargo, dropped 860,320 gallons of water or retardant—1,480 actual flight hours—with no accidents or reports of damaged equipment.

Miscellaneous

The fire cache operated 24 hours a day.

The kitchen was also a 24-hour operation, preparing 800 meals for all of the arriving/departing crews, the jumpers, support personnel, pilots and they also prepared hundreds of meals to either be para-dropped, or delivered via helicopter to personnel on the fires.

Organization

After a few days of chaos Francis and fire management personnel from the regional office and other fire specialists set up an NCSB Organization:

- An Aerial Project Coordinator—Francis Lufkin, who coordinated and managed all aerial project activities, and was a liaison to incoming crews and the community.
- NCSB Air Operations Officer responsible for aircraft safety, regulations, use of aircraft.
- NCSB Safety Officer—general project safety.
- Smokejumper Operations Manager—Bill Moody for dispatch, jumper retrieval, jump plane assignments, jumper assigned aircraft, spotter assignments.

NCSB Para-Rescue Operations, 1957-1989

In the chapter titled, "Challenges of a Rookie Base Manager," I expressed that one was to expand NCSB's capabilities beyond "just a fire service." One expanded capability would be to provide more advanced first-aid capability, a service to benefit both NCSB jumpers and the general recreating public. Dr. Bill Henry was just the man to help us fulfill that objective.

Cooperation: A Doctor, a Sheriff, and Forest Service/NCSB

The purpose of this paper is to provide NCSB and Aero-Methow Rescue with a historical record of the unique partnership developed in the 1960s for expedient backcountry pararescue and medevac.

Since the 1940's the smokejumper program has provided a rapid first responder para-rescue capability to injured jumpers, firefighters, forest personnel and the general recreation public. This capability was highlighted by Dr. Amos Little's heroic jump in 1944 to provide medical care to the flight crew of a crashed B-17 in Colorado.

INFORMAL BACKCOUNTRY SAR AGREEMENT

For many years area physicians felt the need for improved emergency care, for both permanent residents and valley and backcountry visitors. In 1968 NCSB, through an "informal special cooperative agreement" developed a more effective backcountry pararescue response to serve not only smokejumper operations, but also the general recreating public. Partners in this endeavor were the Okanogan National Forest/NCSB, the Okanogan County Sheriff's Department and local primary care physician Dr. William (Doc) Henry, founder of Aero-Methow Rescue. Dr. Henry was an ex-Navy Flight

Surgeon. Dr. James Baker, an ex-Navy helicopter pilot and medical doctor joined Henry's Aero-Methow Rescue team in 1968. During his tenure with Dr. Henry, Dr. Baker completed NCSB jump training in 1969 and 70. Although he never made a pararescue jump, he did make a fire jump on the Wenatchee National Forest in 1970.

Dr. Henry, a nationally recognized leader in backcountry emergency services saw the need for pooling the Okanogan County SAR resources. The Sheriff's Department was not well prepared, or equipped, for backcountry SAR responses. The county is located on the east slope of the North Cascades, much of it is national forest, including the Pasayten and Lake Chelan-Sawtooth Wildernesses. The North Cascades National Park borders the forest on the west and British Columbia forms the northern border. The region has a fairly heavy fire occurrence and very heavy recreation use. Responses to backcountry accidents/illnesses were slow, and often times inadequate.

MISSION PROTOCOLS

The objective of the cooperative agreement was to provide a rapid pararescue medevac response to both Forest Service personnel as well as to forest recreationists. Requests for backcountry SAR services generally came from persons associated with the injured party, or someone aware of the need for medical help, often wilderness rangers. Requests for assistance were made to the Forest Service, or the Sheriff or to Aero-Methow Rescue/Dr. Henry. A simple decision matrix was followed to determine the best first responder resource.

If the decision matrix indicated that jumpers were the most expedient resource to respond the Forest Dispatcher placed a Resource Order with NCSB pending availability of EMTs, daylight requirements, etc. For non-Forest Service personnel, the request would generally come from the Sheriff. When Dr. Henry received a direct request he notified the Sheriff and

Forest Service, often times with a request for the NCSB pararescue team.

The NCSB pararescue team consisted of a Team Leader and multiple EMTs plus additional "litter carriers", if needed. The average number of jumpers per mission was four. A first aid equipment module was always carried on board the jump plane. More specialized emergency gear was loaded on board as "might be needed."

Although most jump conditions were similar to the "average fire jump", several rescues exceeded "fire jump parameters."

Once on the ground the mission protocol called for conducting a medical evaluation, stabilizing the patient, communicating the patient evaluation directly to Dr. Henry, following the doctor's standing orders, determining the most expedient medevac option and transporting the injured via litter/ambulance or helicopter to a medical facility.

The average time from notification to arrival at a medical facility was 5 hours, pending daylight.

When available, Forest Service contract or CWN helicopters provided the medevac to the care facility. When not available, military helicopters from Whidbey Island Naval Base, Fairchild Air Force Base or Yakima Firing (Army) Range provided the medevac service.

NCSB FIRST AID/EMT TRAINING

Until 1972 emergency care skills were generally obtained through the standard smokejumper Red Cross training course. Beginning in 1973, Dr. Henry offered an Emergency Medical Technician (EMT) course for Methow Valley residents. A few NCSB jumpers, including myself, took the course and earned an EMT certification. By the mid 70s NCSB normally had four or more certified EMTs. Through the years the Doc gave the NCSB

EMTs advanced training including IV administration, use of epinephrine, plaster cast administration, MAST trousers, air splints, Demerol, O2 administration, and more.

To facilitate medevac operations a three-section tandem litter was developed by Training Foreman Elmer Neufeld, CJ 44/NCSB 45. The litter was designed to be supported by four litter bearers—two persons tandem in front and two in back. This allowed the rescuers to walk on the trail directly in front and back of the litter. An adjustable shoulder harness attached to the litter. Once on a trail the rescuers could travel at 2.5 to 3 mph.

WINTER SAR OPERATIONS

In 1974, in response to a couple of winter backcountry medevac requests, the Forest authorized winter pararescue/SAR operations.

During the 1970s a US Forest Service Twin Beech was stationed on the Okanogan year around. An Aero Commander was also available.

In preparation for winter jump operations NCSB overhead took a US Air Force Winter Survival course at Fairchild Air Force Base, in Spokane, Washington. During the winters 1974 through 1976 we jumped to six different "winter exercise" locations in the mountains surrounding the Methow Valley, all in snow two feet to six feet in depth. Light weight small snow shoes were carried in the jump pant pocket to facilitate access to the cargo. Full size snow shoes and a snow sled were dropped for patient (jump gear) extrication. On a couple of the training exercises we "overnighted" in igloos/snow shelters. Although the winter SAR capability proved feasible, the Forest/NCSB decided to terminate the program. There were no actual pararescue missions during this time.

WENATCHEE RAPPEL (SMOKESLIDER) TRAINING

During the analysis period the Wenatchee National Forest rappel crews (smokesliders) conducted their annual rappel training at NCSB. If jump conditions precluded jumping, we wanted a backup platform to deploy our pararescue team. Like jumping, rappelling provided quick access to injured persons and met our Cooperative Pararescue/SAR agreement objectives. Each spring NCSBs EMTs, including myself, would go through rappel certification. Although we never used the rappel option on a rescue, we did provide jumpers for a fire.

DR. BRENT SMITH WILDERNESS PARA-RESCUE STUDY

In 1989 Brent A. Smith MD (NCSB 1985), Department of Emergency Medicine at Darnall Army Hospital in Fort Hood, Texas (and ex-RAC, MSO and NCSB jumper) authored a study: "SMOKEJUMPER WILDERNESS RESCUE MISSIONS: Experience of the North Cascades Smokejumper Base: 1957-1988." Report data was obtained from NCSB/Forest Service logs and personal records from 1957 to 1989 (1989 added to Brent's analysis).

Not included in Dr. Smith's analysis are helicopter rescue missions.

NOTE: Brent served 10 years active duty and multiple tours as a frontline doctor. Tours included Desert Storm, Iraq, the Sinai and Afghanistan. As a smokejumper Brent made over 100 fire jumps. Brent passed away in 2018.

During the study period NCSB responded to a wide variety of emergencies involving both Forest Service and non-Forest Service personnel. These included: four aircraft crashes, hunter gunshot incidents, dynamite cap explosion blowing off a hand of a Forest Service employee, two cardiac related incidents, perforated peptic ulcer, multiple horse related broken backs, ribs, pelvis, legs, ankle, diabetics, sepsis (severe blood poisoning), jumper broken backs, broken legs, and dislocated shoulders, pneumothorax, third degree burns, and premature labor.

Four missions involved recovery of deceased victims suffering injuries related to aircraft crashes, a victim of a fatal gunshot wound and a fatal horse rollover.

We applied CPR, administered IVs, epinephrine to a lookout suffering anaphylaxis, plaster casts, lots of Demerol, many splints, neck braces, backboards, packed out a "freeze dried" glacier hiker, missing for seven years, and conducted a 20-jumper two-day search for a lost hiker on the Canadian border.

WILDERNESS RESCUE REPORT FINDINGS

Dr. Smith's study documented NCSB jumpers responding to 62 pararescue/SAR missions from 1957 to 1988. There were a couple of additional para-rescues in 1989. Dr. Smith's report included only "parachute missions" although NCSB did respond to a handful of helicopter and vehicle access requests. The analysis revealed that from 1957-1988, 18% of the rescues were classified in the "critical or fatal outcome" category, 67.5% classified as "urgent" and 8.5 % classified as "trauma." Dr. Smith determined that 45% of the victims were transported to a care facility primarily by helicopter, 18% primarily via litter. Half of the victims were Forest Service employees, the other half were civilians, generally recreationists.

EPILOGUE

Doc Henry distinguished himself in emergency medicine. He developed state-level EMT training programs and guidelines. Doc retired in 1990 and passed away in 1998. Aero-Methow Rescue continues under the very able leadership of Dr. Henry's daughter and paramedic, Cindy Button. Aero-Methow is recognized for its outstanding service and is a critical part of EMS in the Methow Valley and Okanogan County.

After leaving Aero-Methow in 1970 Dr. Baker returned to school to become a pathologist and reenlisted in the Navy. He is now retired.

Dr. Brent Smith had a distinguished career serving multiple tours of duty in major Middle East war zones. Brent passed away in 2018.

During his career Base Manager Bill Moody made 31 pararescue/search jumps.

NCSB continues to have a cadre of EMTs and a paramedic available to serve the smokejumper community and the public.

Doc Henry's vision lives on.

Jumpin' with the Russkies in East Siberia

In the chapter titled, "National and International Opportunities," I wrote about my trip to the Soviet Union in 1976 during the Cold War as part of the U.S.-Soviet Technical Exchange Program. A part of the exchange called for me to make parachute jumps with the Soviet smokejumpers. This article documents my two jumps with my Russian counterparts.

During October 1976 Doug Bird (ex-McCall jumper and Washington Office Fire Management), interpreter Alex Vasilevsky and I participated in the US-USSR Scientific-Technical Exchange Program. In addition to being a seasoned jumper and base manager I was also a qualified and current helicopter rappeler. Although we were interested in the entire Soviet jump and rappel programs, our primary objective was to evaluate the Russian Lesnik "Forester" parachute—a 28-foot multi-porosity round parachute with D-bag, with good maneuvering characteristics.

The "Lesnik" is basically a freefall system. To activate the deployment sequence the jumper attaches a 4 ft. static line to the overhead cable. Upon exiting the aircraft, the 4 ft. static line pulls out a drogue, or stabilizing chute which stabilizes the jumper as he/she falls. After a 5 second freefall the jumper pulls the ripcord and the main chute is deployed, aided by the drag of the drogue chute. At the time the US forest Service was looking for a replacement for the FS-10 parachute and the BLM was developing their Ram Air, square system.

Upon arriving in Irkutsk, East Siberia (location of the regional aerial base) I received basic jump training which consisted of parachute manipulation, letdown procedures, exits, and landing rolls. I was scheduled to make two jumps—one with all US gear/FS-10 and one jump with all Soviet gear except for my

White's boots. The jumps were scheduled to be held in Ust-Ilimsk, Air Base, a small base located on the Angara River about 400 miles north of Irkutsk. About twelve or so supervisory jumpers from throughout the east Siberia/Irkutsk Region would be involved in this first American-Soviet smokejumper event, "an international jump off." Through some means they selected Mikal Bocharov to make the first jump with the Americanski.

The morning of the jump we and the pilots, all gathered at the jump shack for the required pre-jump physical. The physical, administered by a cute blonde female doctor, consisted of taking my pulse, blood pressure, observing the eyes and apparently an evaluation of the breath for indication of alcohol consumption. The "physical" was certified by recording the event in the registration book. In the mean time workers were shoveling out a pile of potatoes from the interior of the jump plane. The jump plane was an AN-2, a 1930s vintage bi-wing with a reciprocal radial engine, the backbone of the Soviet smokejumper fleet. After a ground equipment check we boarded the plane and the jump door was shut—and would remain so until on final and about five seconds before exit. Except for Doug, no one spoke English. I had to observe and make a logical guess as to the jump procedures.

Once airborne we climbed to their standard jump altitude, 3,000 feet above a nearby meadow, Neven's Field. The first snow of the year occurred over night—we would jump onto a four-inch layer of snow. As we reached altitude the spotter (pilot-observer) directed the pilot's flight line from the co-pilot's seat, a standard practice. The streamers were let out over the release point and the plane made a right-hand pattern. I "read the streamers" as we orbited—good wind, estimated at about 600 yards of drift. The spotter and assistant near the exit door were explaining the streamers to the Russkies, but Doug and I didn't have a clue what they were saying. The spotter decided to throw a second "confirmation set of streamers"—they were right on. I hooked up to the over head cable, got behind the Russkie as we lined out on final. On final our air speed was 93 mph. Soon the assistant opened the jump door, five seconds later we exited into the icy blast.

The spotter had us on wind line and we maneuvered the long trek back to the X marker on the ground, me on an FS-10 and Mikal on a Lesnik. We both landed about 15 feet from the center of the X—shook hands—both extremely proud of the accomplishment and the honor we brought to our respective jump programs and to our country. I was the first American smokejumper to jump in the Soviet Union. Equally important was the feeling of "smokejumper comradeship"—a Russkie and an Americanski in the midst of the great cold war.

I found out shortly after we landed that my interpreter Alex had bet against me being closest to the spot because my FS-10 was inferior to the Soviet Lesnik. It was a "tie"—and we drank several vodka toasts that night to the Soviet and American jumper programs. The following day I jumped the Lesnik in Soviet gear. It was windy again but I managed to land close to the X with the top Russkies—another evening of toasts to the brotherhood.

A side note to the exchange. In 1977 the Soviets visited the United States and made a jump with us at NCSB. They left one of their Lesnik "Forester" parachutes and Soviet jump gear. The canopy, with a few modifications, became our new FS-12 chute. We did not adopt the Soviet "freefall system" and would continue with a static line deployment system. The drogue chute from the Lesnik was sent to the Alaska BLM and was incorporated into their Ram Air square system. The primary objective was achieved!

The Soviet exchange was certainly one of the highlights of my career and I am honored that I could represent my country and the US jumper program.

Hard Landings Can Make You Shorter

In the chapter titled, "National and International Opportunities," I wrote about "The Jump That Made Me Shorter." The following article appeared in the National Smokejumper Association magazine a few years ago. Used by permission.

In June 1957, before rookie jumps, I was 6' 0" tall, "a proud 6-footer." By the end of August, 1978, I was 6' on one side and 5' 10.5" on the other. By 1983 I "measured in" on both sides, at 5' 10.5". It's true, after years of hard landings, jumping can make you shorter. Now, "the rest of the story."

In August 1978, after receiving a complaint from a District Ranger that the jumpers on the 4th of July Basin Fire (Devore Creek) had buried their garbage rather than pack it out, I decided to make an "investigative/PR jump" to check things out.

The fire was five plus acres and was staffed by NCSB and jumpers from other bases. After five days the fire was declared out and the crew prepared for a nine-mile pack out to the head of Lake Chelan. To lighten the pack out weight the garbage accumulated over the five days was burned, put in plastic garbage bags and buried two feet deep some distance away from the campsite.

A day after the jumpers left the fire a "duty-bound wilderness ranger" decided to check the fire for "wilderness compliance." After searching the fire area he found some disturbed soil, dug down two feet and found a plastic bag full of burned garbage. The sack of evidence was delivered to the District Ranger. The Ranger subsequently called me to report the wilderness ranger's findings. We agreed to meet after I checked things out.

Early in the morning of August 29th members of the "rogue garbage crew incident" and I jumped in to 4th of July Basin (6,000') in the Glacier Peak Wilderness on the Wenatchee National Forest. It was an early morning jump. The rising sun had not reached the basin jump spot—still getting downslope wind. I was jumping an FS-10 chute. On my final turn I encountered a severe downdraft and "smoked in" from over 200 feet, my right femur impacting a rock on the side slope. My femur, just below the hip socket, was shattered in four or five pieces. I was medevacked to Wenatchee Central Washington Hospital where I received seven units of blood. A titanium rod and two plastic bands were used to reconstruct the bone fragments (rod removed a couple years later).

I was on my back in a hospital bed for eleven weeks, five and a half in the hospital, five and a half at home on partial "work status." I spent the next thirteen weeks on crutches. During the PT it was discovered that the restructuring of the "bone fragment puzzle" and healing resulted in a loss of an inch and a half of bone length. To compensate for the shortage I put an inch and a half "lift" on my Whites, cowboy boots and my running shoes. Within seven months I was back running, not very gracefully, but running. I discovered that the bone shortage was causing a lot of ankle and knee discomfort and it was sure to mess up my back before too long. Unhappy about the prospects of not being to maintain my active jumper lifestyle, I was looking for a solution to being "lop sided."

That solution started over a glass of champagne (then a couple more) at Bob Brownlee's (NC-76) wedding and a conversation with Craig Brownlee (NC-76), an orthopedic surgeon finishing his internship at Mayo Clinic. I asked Craig about a way to lengthen my "short leg." Craig explained that the lengthening procedure was a long and somewhat painful procedure, but there is a new procedure to shorten the femur. The new procedure was developed by an orthopedic surgeon who was finishing his residency at Harbor View Hospital in Seattle. After a consultation the following week I gave a big "10-4" to the procedure and I headed for Seattle to get "evened up."

Here's how it works:

1. I received a spinal so I could watch the procedure, along with the doctors, on a fluoroscope monitor.
2. An incision is made on the buttocks at the head of the femur of the "good leg."
3. Bone marrow is removed from the femur and a small saw with a retractable blade is inserted into the femur to the point where the bone is to be severed.
4. The bone is severed (the saw cutting from inside to outside of the bone) a second severe one and a quarter inches below the first.
5. Next, a bone fracturing device is inserted into the femur adjacent to the severed block. In a "mini-explosion" the device shatters the bone fragment into four quadrants, displacing the four pieces just enough to allow the femur to be brought back together.
6. The femur ends are brought together with the quadrant of bone fragments eventually forming a reinforced calcified "collar of bone" around the point where the bone ends were brought together.
7. A metal rod is inserted inside the femur, the full length of femur (removed a couple of years later).
8. Physical therapy the next day and released.
9. I left Harborview Hospital at 5'10.5 inches tall. I left a "pack out bag of pride" there! But I was "evened-up."
10. Five weeks later, back running.
11. Back jumping a couple of months later with rod in leg. I jumped one or two seasons with the rod in my femur.

Both of the rods are now on a plaque on my office wall.

In year 2022 I'm still running, skiing and hiking—life is good. Now you know "the rest of the story"—hard landings can, in fact, make you shorter.

An Old Jumper Reminisces

"Da ya remember those World War II rats—lima beans, pound cake and Lucky Strike cigarettes, yah, and those fish net dinners we had in the 1970s...

"I remember jumping a 28 on a hot day, boy, did I smoke in... before the D-bag, if I had bad position, I ended up with abrasions on my clavicle and a sore neck... on a calm morning you could hear those 28s open up at the Bear Creek training jump spot four miles away..."

When old jumper friends get together, the conversation quickly gravitates to "the good ole days... remember when..." A bit of embellishment made the story a tad bit better, and perhaps, a bit more unbelievable.

After a recent "old jumper conversation" I sat down and began to reminisce about jumping in the 50s and 80s and all that changed—crew composition, hiring and firing practices, jump related equipment, parachutes, fire packs, aircraft, fire suppression operations, pay and other aspects of the program. I assume that you also experienced significant program changes during your career.

Each decade of the jump program saw significant changes, and the program continues to change. This piece spans the mid 50s through 1989, a period that saw significant program changes. For the most part, these were "the good ole days."

THE JUMPERS

Who They Were

The WW II and Korean War vets, and the CPS jumpers of the late 40s and early 50s were gradually replaced by more college bound rookies putting themselves through four years of college—jump four years, get a degree and get "a real job."

Recruits in the 50s-60s were often seasoned farm boys with one or two seasons of fire experience—but they were hard workers with practical woods and mechanical equipment skills.

In the 70s there was a transition to recruits with extensive fire experience, many with college degrees. Jumper tenure was much longer, facilitated by ending of the draft in 1973 and longer term WAE appointments. After the fire season some worked on projects taking advantage of jumper climbing or prescribed burning skills—some hunting, skiing and worldly travels.

Francis B. Lufkin (NC-40)

Francis was the Aerial Project Officer (APO) of the Okanogan Aerial Project, renamed North Cascades Smokejumper Base in 1967. The APO pretty much had control of the hiring and firing. Francis gained fame as one of the original 1939 experimental pioneers, a man bred during the 1920-30s Great Depression. Both feared, and admired, his expectations were high. Francis had an uncanny ability "to size up his jumpers." If you didn't measure up, or if you screwed up "you could be sent down the road kicking horse turds." If you were "salvageable" you were given another chance to prove your worth. As Lufkin counseled a wayward jumper, using the analogy of a bad bear. "When you have a bad bear in camp it is sometimes necessary to shoot it to get rid of it." Or as he "counseled" rookie Gino after a night of partying, "Gino, you're spittin' in the wind." Gino survived, his partner in crime, with previous offenses, didn't! No HR in those days!

Jumper Salary

In 1957 pay for the GS-5 rookie was $1.79/hr. with overtime paid at the same rate. On days off, if there was a T-storm in progress, and anticipating "jumper fires", we were expected to standby without pay. Once a jumper request was made we went on "pay status", at straight pay.

By the time messhall and bunkhouse deductions were calculated you might clear $2,500 for the fire season. The prestige of being a smokejumper, the experiences you had and the guys you worked with primed you for another season.

Thanks to efforts by the Missoula jumper's union in the late 60s, time and a half was initiated along with Hazard Pay, Sunday Differential, and other employee benefits. The age 40 policy restriction was lifted and jumpers could jump until mandatory retirement, providing they could pass the PT test adopted in 1969.

Standard attire in the 50s was either Levi or Frisco jeans, stagged! If the jumper did not stag his new pants, the crew would do the honors for him. The work shirt, was a standard long sleeved work shirt. Whites were the jump boot of choice. You broke them in by wading in the irrigation ditch running through the base and wearing the boots all day or until they felt dry.

PPE

By the mid 1960s the orange fire resistant shirt was standard. A yellow shirt, more distinguishable from fire flames, soon replaced the orange shirt.

Fiberglass hard hats replaced metal hard hats.

By the early 70s the Frisco/Levi jeans were replaced with standard fire Nomex pants. Thus, introduction of the smokejumper "black leg syndrome."

The 3.5 pound fire shelter was adopted as a standard "must carry."

JUMP TRAINING

Rookie training was 4-4.5 weeks, with seven training jumps. Refresher training was usually 3-5 days with two "refresher" jumps. After a couple of weeks without a fire jump we got a refresher jump. Throughout the season we did PT twice a day, including running the 1.5 mile around the airport in our Whites. By the 70s running shoes were permitted.

The Torture Rack—its value was questionable. Some old timers attribute their "back problem" to the torture rack. By 1970 the torture rack was gone without anyone coming to its defense.

JUMPER RELATED GEAR

The Jump Suit

 In 1960 the 1950s cotton canvas fabric jump suit was replaced with nylon fabric with high density foam padding. After a few years the combustibility of the nylon suit was recognized and its use terminated. Nomex, and later Kevlar, materials replaced nylon.

Jump Helmets

In the late 50s and early 60s we had a mix of old classic leather football and plastic football helmets. By the 70s the Bell motorcycle type helmet replaced the football helmets.

Jumper Communications

The yellow signal streamers, later dayglo pink, was the primary communications with the jumper or observation aircraft and forest headquarters. Radios were at a premium.

The 5-Watt and 10-Watt radios weighed several pounds and were dropped on a 10-12 ft. chute—more weight and bulk to packout. The radio's channel was the Forest's primary channel or an Air Net frequency. The compact 9600 Channel King personal portable radio introduced in the 70s greatly improved the communications between the jumper, jump plane and forest headquarters. The signal streamer continued to be a secondary means of communications—you still put out an "L" to indicate a safe landing.

THE FIRE PACK

The basic contents of the fire pack, hand tools and subsistence items, except for food, changed little from the 50s to 80s.

The primary jumper tools were the Pulaski and fire shovel.

In the 1950s chainsaws were a luxury tool with only two chainsaws in our inventory in 1957. The standard "falling tool" was still the Pulaski or cross-cut saw. Gradually, each year, we added more chainsaws. By the mid 70s we had a chainsaw for every jumper.

From the WW II "C-rats", consisting of Lima Beans, SPAM, a small fruit pound cake and a pack of Lucky Strike cigarettes, the fire pack food gradually improved. We experimented with different innovative food packs. Through the years we were introduced to post 1958 "upgraded" rations, the "fish-net" breakfasts and dinners, requiring boiling, Vietnam era MREs, and different freeze-dry foods.

CLIMBING GEAR

During the 50s and 60s the climbing gear consisted of a length of rope cut from the letdown rope, the main parachute tray belt with D-rings, and a tree branch. The section of letdown rope, depending on the circumference of the tree, was tied to the D-ring on the tray belt. A slim smooth tree branch was inserted into the tubular nylon jump rope and the end of the rope was attached to the other D-ring on the tray belt. The inserted branch formed a rigid semi-hoop and would serve to advance the rope up on the backside of the tree. This innovative use of jump rope, tray belt and a branch did not instill much confidence in the tree climbing operation.

The standard "professional climbing equipment" introduced in the 70s greatly improved our confidence in tree climbing.

PARACHUTES

Pre-D-Bag Era

The chutes were the Derry slotted FS-2 candy striped (or white) 28-footer, or for the heavy weights, the 32-foot FS-5A canopy. The canopy was accordion folded on the tray and covered with a bungee cover. The apex of the chute was attached to the end of the static line with a 120 lb. break-cord. The deployment sequence resulted in relatively hard opening shock. Poor body position, on your side or head down position, would result in harness burns on the clavicles, occasional loss of helmet, riser or shroud line neck abrasions, and one hell of a sore neck. On one occasion, on a fire jump, the opening knocked the jumper out for about 60 seconds, waking just before impact.

Line-overs were fairly common, and there was an occasional perfect "Mae West."

By 1962 the D-bag was adopted and by 1965 the 28-footer was phased out.

The D-bag greatly reduced both the opening shock and malfunctions. In about 1978 the addition of the AIN (anti inversion netting) almost completely eliminated malfunctions.

Remembering Those 28s

I remember those 28s for two reasons—the hard openings and hard landings. At 180 lbs., on a hot day, on the Unity District of the Wallowa-Whitman I numbed the bottom of my feet and popped the shoe laces on my Whites.

The Toggle Guideline

In the early 70s the two guidelines attached to the rear riser were shortened. Wooden toggles were added to the end of the guideline. A small pouch on the riser stowed the toggle until opening. The toggle allowed for better guideline access and control of maneuvering during the descent.

The FS-10 and FS-12 Chutes

In 1970 we began the transition from the Derry slotted 28s and 32s to the parabolic FS-10 (T-10) with deployment bag. AIN was added in 1977.

Modeled after the Soviet Forester smokejumper chute design, in 1980 the Forest Service adopted the 32- foot multi-porosity steerable FS-12 with a deployment bag.

SMOKEJUMPER AIRCRAFT: FROM RECIPS TO TURBINES

The Noorduyn—that old 600 horse power beast could be heard 30 plus miles away, lumbering along at 138 mph. The jump door was on the right side.

In 1957 NCSB's primary jump plane was a Noorduyn Norseman with a "back up" contract Twin Beech, contracted primarily for the La Grande spike operations.

In 1958 NCSB upgraded to a USFS Twin Beech. On June 23, 1958 N164Z crashed on Eight Mile Ridge, killing the pilot Bob Cavanaugh, Supervisory Smokejumper   Keith Hendrickson, and jumpers Gerald Helmer and Robert Carlman, a jump qualified forester.

Eventually, NCSB upgraded to a Forest Service DC-3, N168Z. In the 70s a Beech 99A replaced the Twin Beech. An Aero Commander "general utility" backup platform was used at NCSB in the 70s and 80s.

In the 1980s NCSB had a contract Beech 99A and later, contract Twin Otters.

FIRE OPERATIONS

Aggressive initial attack began with Lufkin's 7-minute "wheels up" policy. The suit-up procedure was speeded up when Titus (Bill) Nelson (NC-66) developed a "speed rack" with pre-connected gear—simply slip-in to the gear mounted on the rack, attach the three harness straps, secure the reserve, and proceed to the spotter checkout.

During periods of moderate and high fire danger the Okanogan and Wenatchee National Forests employed an "automatic jumper dispatch" policy. As soon as a fire was reported jumpers were launched.

The program was successful but abandoned when the newer fire staffing guidelines were adopted.

Jumper patrols were standard operations after lightning storms and during periods of high fire danger. When NCSB flew Forest Service Working Capital Fund (WCF) aircraft it was standard practice to "fly off" the daily two-hour WCF time on evening standby.

1970 FIRE SEASON: NCSB RECORD YEAR

1970 was almost a continuous fire bust with endless mini and mega lightning storms from early June to late September. For a 10-day period NCSB exceeded Spokane International in terms of takeoffs and landings—325 daily. During the July bust 176 jumpers worked out of NCSB. It was a 24-hour operation, serving over 800 meals a day out of the messhall. We ended the season with 1066 jumps on 212 fires out of NCSB and 213 jumps on 64 fires out of our satellite base at La Grande.

AGGRESSIVE FIRE CONTAINMENT

Once on the ground the standard game plan was to fight the fire aggressively until achieving containment, sometimes doing an "all-nighter", taking advantage of the cooler temperatures and higher relative humidity. The aggressive initial attack containment objective resulted in preventing "jumper fires" from becoming major incidents—a novel concept!

PACKBOARDS TO PACKOUT BAGS

The standard jumper pack in the 1950s, early 60s was a WWII military pack board, two seamless Bemis grain sacks to stuff your gear in, and innertube rubber bands to secure the Bemis sacks on to the backboard.

Later, from Lufkin's military surplus source, we modified military canvas bags ("the Elephant Bag") by adding shoulder straps.

By the 80s we manufactured well designed packout bags from lighter materials, with adjustable load straps.

PROGRAM SURVIVAL

Predictions of Phase Out

With increased helicopter use and the introduction of helitack and helijumpers in the 50s, and rappelling in the 70s, the question was, and continues to be, what's the future of the jump program? Rumor had it that helitack would take over, and jumpers would be obsolete in the late 60s. With the introduction of rappelling in 1973 a similar prediction was made and the jump program days were numbered.

NCSB Base Studies

NCSB has been the victim of a half dozen plus studies to determine if it should remain a permanent base, a seasonal base or an occasionally used spike base. After a national base study in 1978, the national and regional office targeted NCSB to become a Region 6 satellite or spike base.

In the early 80s the Regional Office all but terminated the NCSB program.

Stripped of Chutes and Sewing Machines

NCSB could no longer rig chutes or manufacture jump related equipment at NCSB. All of the sewing machines were transferred to Redmond, except for a couple we "rat holed." After chutes were jumped they had to be sent to Redmond for repacking and repairs.

NCSB Staffing

Staffing was reduced to 11 jumpers. With support of the Forest Supervisor, we hired one fully qualified ex-NCSB CWN jumper and four "blue chip" fully qualified volunteers (paid when assigned to a fire). They were great jumpers and appreciated the opportunity "to get their foot in the door." When NCSB regained permanent status in 1984, three of the four were hired as regular jumpers.

RAC Spike Base at Wenatchee

The Region set up a spike jumper operation out of Wenatchee, 65 airline miles from NCSB. Jumper dispatches for fires in the North Cascades, even within sight of NCSB, were dispatched from Wenatchee. Okanogan Dispatch dispatched NCSB to some "Okanogan fires."

Saved From Extinction

During this dark period Forest Supervisor Bill McLaughlin (MSO -58), along with Washington senators, representatives, state and local politicians rallied on NCSB's behalf to maintain NCSB as a permanent base. Supported by a comprehensive 1984 Region 6 smokejumper program study, headed up by Ken Snell (MSO-67) Region 6 Fire Management, the decision was made to maintain NCSB as a permanent base with 21 jump personnel. Parachutes, along with "rigging privileges" and sewing machines were returned and normal operations resumed.

NCSB's Future

The 2015 base study appeared to support keeping NCSB as a permanent base with upgraded facilities and 30 jumpers. As of this writing there has been no progress on upgrading the facilities.

What does the future hold for NCSB, and for the national smokejumper program?

Israel's Mount Carmel Fire

In 2010 and 2016 the 747 Supertanker was dispatched to Tel Aviv, Israel to fight wildland fires. The following article is about our 2010 response to fight the 12,500-acre Mt. Carmel Fire near Haifa, a fire that took forty-two lives.

The world's largest airtanker, Evergreen's 747 "Tanker 979," launched from Marana, Arizona, for Tel Aviv, Israel, Dec. 3, 2010, to fight modern Israel's largest fire ever—the Carmel Fire. The fire would claim 42 lives and burn 12,500 acres of Israel's Carmel Forest near Haifa.

Tanker 979's drops would make a significant contribution in stopping the spread of the fire and signal the beginning of rapid, effective airtanker global response—and smokejumpers were a part of this history. The "jumper connection" story involves former and current smokejumpers, an ex-smokejumper pilot, and a smokejumper documentary videographer.

A New Paradigm in Airtanker Operations

The Boeing 747 airtanker concept was "conceived" by Evergreen International Aviation founder and president, Del Smith, in 1985. After two fatal Forest Service-contracted airtanker crashes in 2002, Smith—with the encouragement of Evergreen 747 pilot Cliff Hale—felt the time was right to move ahead with developing a new paradigm in aerial firefighting: a 747 "supertanker."

Today the 747 is technically referred to in the Incident Command System as a VLAT, or Very Large Air Tanker. There are only two under contract in the U.S.: the Evergreen 747 and 10 Tanker Air Carrier's DC-10.

After two years of engineering and the development of an internal pressurized tanking system, the prototype 747 was ready for flight-testing.

The Jumper Connection

From 2002 to 2008 the tanker underwent rigorous testing and crew training, with two ex-smokejumpers and a former smokejumper pilot heavily involved in the drop-system development and retardant pilot training.

You never know when past associations, experiences, and people you've worked with in the national smokejumper program might re-enter your life and lead to exciting opportunities. It's not often you get an opportunity to be part of a new paradigm in your professional career.

In late 2003 a call from ex-smokejumper pilot Penn Stohr, Jr. — who served as a Johnson Flying Service smokejumper pilot from the 1960s to 1975—then Evergreen's chief pilot and senior vice president of operations, changed it all. Stohr, along with Hale, would be Supertanker Project Co-Managers from 2003 to 2006.

Penn's call to me, a current Air Tactical Group supervisor, and Nels Jensen (MSO-62), an ex-lead plane pilot and current contract smokejumper pilot at Grangeville, was met with a "What? A 747 dropping retardant?"

Jensen and I looked at it as another smokejumper challenge— "people will think I'm nuts to be involved in a harebrained scheme for dropping retardant from a 747."

Two jumpers have joined me and Jensen in the Supertanker legacy—videographer Eric Hipke (NCSB-90) and Jamie Tackman (NCSB-75), who was also a lead plane pilot from 1994 until 2010.

Hipke assisted videographer Steve Smith (Associate), ex-NSA historian and producer of our smokejumper documentary "Firefighters From the Sky," with filming the 747 operational flight evaluations in the mountains north of Marana, Arizona.

Smith has produced several evaluation documentaries and marketing videos for Evergreen since the project began. Tackman was one of the two U.S. Forest Service lead plane pilots assigned to "lead" and evaluate performance of the Supertanker during the 2006 mountainous terrain evaluation—the SOAP (Supertanker Operations Assessment Project).

Kevin Meekin, Region 1 lead plane pilot, was the other SOAP evaluation pilot.

The Tasks

In addition to developing an aircraft capable of dropping 20,000 gallons of retardant, the program required training the 747 flight crews to fly low-level retardant missions. Because of his low-level smokejumper cargo drop and fire fighting background, Stohr was given the responsibility for training 747 flight crews to industry standards.

To accomplish this, Evergreen (Stohr) hired me and Jensen to do the air attack-related basic and advanced training. Jensen, with his smokejumper pilot and lead plane background and a season of retardant flying under his belt, was selected to train the flight crews in low-level mountain flying. Together, Jensen and I evaluated the drop system and advised on how best to use the aircraft in tactical operations.

Tanker 979 Heavy Ready For Action

The Supertanker, as Evergreen refers to it, is a 20,000-gallon airtanker with a pressurized constant-flow drop system. The system consists of 10 liquid-agent tanks and eight air-pressure tanks. The agents—water, foam, gel or long-term retardant—are expelled through one or more of the four 16-inch nozzles located in the belly of the aircraft.

The flight engineer regulates the air pressure, number of tanks and nozzles to achieve the desired concentration or coverage level. The pilot releases the load by depressing a button on his yoke. The 747 is capable of dropping the entire load in one drop or multiple segmented drops.

The Supertanker is currently on a call-when-needed contract to the U.S. Forest service and Cal Fire. In 2009 and 2010 Tanker 979 flew on one fire in Alaska and three fires in southern California.

An International Response

On the afternoon of Dec. 2, the Supertanker was requested by the Israeli government to assist in fighting a person-caused (14-year-old boy smoking a water pipe) wildfire southeast of Haifa. The region was in a seven-year drought and had a very hot and dry summer and fall. Shortly after the Carmel Fire broke out, there were 20 arson attempts resulting in four arrests. The fires were quickly suppressed.

On Dec. 3, the Supertanker—with the three-person flight crew, two mechanics, an avionics technician and me—launched on a 15-hour flight from Marana, Arizona, to Tel Aviv, Israel, via John F. Kennedy Airport in New York. We would join a total of 18 nations (some of them Muslim) that committed air and ground resources for the suppression and relief effort. Twenty-seven helicopters and airtankers were involved.

The fire made some major runs that afternoon and evening, as we were en route over the Atlantic Ocean. We arrived in Tel Aviv's Ben Gurion International Airport about 1 a.m., Dec. 5, slept briefly, received a briefing the next morning, and launched on one of two sorties.

166

I prepared a briefing document and requested information that we needed to fly safe and effective missions.

Israel does not have a wildland fire-suppression program—no initial attack crews, no shot crews, no airtankers, no lead planes, no ICS. They fought the fire with local fire brigades and their engines. Except for wet lines near structures, fires were not lined, as they don't have hand crews. Sixty U.S. firefighters, including 12 NCSB jumpers and hotshot crews, were activated for deployment, but the order was later canceled when containment was declared.

The flight crews of the 27 foreign airtankers and helicopters—speaking different languages—required a number of interpreters on board the military traffic-control aircraft and the respective airtankers and medium/heavy helicopters.

The airtankers included a Russian Ilyushin 76, a 10,000-gallon water-dropping airtanker, and two BE 200, 3,000-gallon scooper aircraft.

Other airtankers included CL-415 water scoopers and single-engine airtankers from Spain, Italy, Greece, Turkey, Cyprus, France and Bulgaria. Local fire brigade teams mixed the retardant sent in from France—Fire Trol 931, a liquid retardant concentrate. The Israeli mixing team, assisted by the Evergreen ground crew, loaded the Supertanker in 22 minutes, slightly faster than the usual 25 minutes required to load the 747.

The fleet of foreign airtankers did a very effective and professional job. As a result of their efforts and with a moderation in fire behavior the night of Dec. 5, the fast-moving fire front subsided before it could spread into the housing developments situated within the Carmel Forest area. Our drops were placed along the smoldering unlined fire perimeter to protect these housing developments. As far as I know the perimeters were never lined.

The First Sortie

The first Supertanker load was with water and what was left of a small quantity of liquid retardant—just enough to give the load a faint pink color. A large shipment of retardant arrived shortly after the tanker was loaded.

After a "brief briefing," Tanker 979 launched for the Carmel Fire, about 15 minutes to the north. On board were two Israeli Air Force officers, including a two-star general. They were to help identify the drop area, interpret and interact with the air traffic controller over the fire.

Upon arrival in the drop area, a Russian BE 200 scooper was just finishing a drop. The Supertanker, along with the Russian IL 76 and four CL-415 water scoopers, were put into orbit by the military air space controller. The Supertanker orbits and drop were tracked live on Israeli TV. Once cleared to drop, Tanker 979 did a split load of two drops along the smoldering fire perimeter. The objective was to protect adjacent structures. The drops appeared very effective. The mission went smoothly.

Sortie No. 2

I was supposed to ride with the air traffic control officer (military), operating from a different airport, but somehow, due to scheduling, that didn't work out. Two Israeli Air Force officers and I flew on the second 747 flight. I was an "on-board air attack" to confirm the target and placement of the drop.

Israel does not have an air attack coordinating drops and giving target instructions. The target information comes from a ground firefighter requesting a drop at a specific GPS waypoint. The coordinates are called to the air base, and the airtanker is deployed. The pilot has to figure out the drop start and stop points. I'm not sure how they deal with "new higher priorities."

The second load was a direct wet line—this time of full-strength LC retardant—on the smoldering perimeter to check the spread into a major housing development. The drop was more than a mile long at a medium coverage level; it went well.

The Prime Minister's Visit

Prime Minister Benjamin Netanyahu visited the 747 operation in the evening for about an hour. It was a major media event with mega-security. He was given a tour of the 747. I had about five minutes, "one-on-one," with him regarding retardant use and then attended a debriefing, where he asked me about retardant's ability to extinguish the fire. I told him it doesn't extinguish the fire, but will impede its advance.

Netanyahu is a very impressive and commanding individual—sharp, personable, well-informed, and asked very insightful questions.

The Aftermath

In the days following the fire's containment, there was major political fallout about Israel's lack of preparedness. The prime minister has vowed to develop an effective fire-suppression program, including an airtanker program.

The Carmel Fire killed 42 people, including 41 prison guards and police and a young firefighter. The fire burned 12,500 acres (about 45 percent) of their Carmel Forest—one of the very few forested areas in Israel. This was the largest wildfire in Israel's 62-year history as a modern nation.

Our part in fighting the Carmel Fire and working internationally with the 747 was a great experience. The opportunity to participate with 27 aircraft from 13 nations, speaking 13 languages, working cooperatively and effectively together, without any previous international training was extremely satisfying. It is equally satisfying to see how "the smokejumper connection" contributed to the success of the mission.

Two Fools Jump into Three Fools Pass

As trained EMTs, John Button and I responded to several search and rescue calls. One of the most memorable calls was a late-evening (almost dark) jump we made to administer aid to an injured horseman.

During my smokejumper career I made over thirty search and rescue jumps to aid fellow jumpers, Forest Service employees, pilots, and backcountry recreationists. Missions included all sorts of broken bones and dislocations, heart attacks, bee sting, diabetic issues, serious foot/leg infection, severe shock/collapsed lung, perforated peptic ulcer, gun-shot hunters, aircraft crashes, searches and body recovery of a dehydrated, very long over due, glacier explorer—and more.

Thanks to the leadership and training we received from Dr. Bill Henry, founder of Aero-Methow Rescue, NCSB jumpers received advanced first aid/EMT training to prepare us for rescuing not only our jumpers but also others needing expedient emergency care and transport to a medical facility. NCSB's para-rescue teams have responded to probably 80-100 emergencies since the 40s. Many of these were "supervised" by Doc Henry from his Twisp Medical Center office—communicating directly, or via the jump plane, with the jumper in charge of the rescue.

Perhaps due to the urgency of the response we often "pushed the envelope" with regard to wind, terrain, and visibility conditions. Many of the rescue jumps I made were among the most difficult of my career due to the adverse jump conditions.

We arrived over the Three Fools Pass area north of Billy Goat Pass in the Pasayten Wilderness Area about 2120 on July 28, 1980—and it was just about dark. Our mission was to find, then jump, to give emergency aid to a seriously injured horseman. Three Fools Pass was appropriately named—one fool, the horseman who tried unsuccessfully to pull his stubborn horse across a foot bridge and in the process fell on to the stream bed below shattering his ankle—and the two fools about to jump in the dark to rescue fool number one. I was somewhat familiar with Three Fools Pass as I had carried an injured hiker on a litter through Three Fools Pass a few years earlier.

As Dale Deardon, pilot of the Beech 99, circled the area we picked up a camp fire about 300-400 yards north of the pass— good enough for us—it had to be the injured horseman's. With barely a silhouette on the horizon spotter Bob Kinyon threw a set of streamers (which we could occasionally barely see). We made a half-assed guess that we had about 100-200 yards of drift. We hooked up and got in the door. The jump was going to be a timber jump into the pass area. The next run, at 2125, John and I exited and had a quick descent toward the pass using the campfire as reference. The pass and trees were an almost indistinguishable silhouette. As I made my approach for landing in the pass I tried extra hard to be relaxed, knowing the pass also had lots of rock. I bombed into a bushy 30-40 foot tree along side the trail and stepped out of my harness. John, second out, and with little time to maneuver, landed about a hundred yards away in the short timber. Due to the conditions, we decided not to drop Steve Pontarolo and Tom King. We would be bringing in a helicopter to the pass area for the medevac in the morning and would not have to transport the injured via litter to the trail head.

Pilot Deardon maintained a safe and conservative flight pattern while Kinyon dropped the para-rescue gear in the pass area. All went well, we retrieved the cargo and headed down the trail to find a grateful and hurting horseman. He had indeed fallen about five feet into a dry rocky creek bed. After a quick assessment we relayed our findings, via the jump plane, to Doc Henry— "a seriously injured horseman, probably shattered ankle." Doc's protocol instructed us to straighten the ankle as best we could then administer a plaster cast, a skill we had recently learned from Doc. The procedure went well and much of the pain was relieved. I believe we also administered a shot of Demerol to curb the pain.

At about 2400 I returned to the pass and scouted for a helicopter landing area. A suitable landing area requiring little improvement was located on the south side of the pass. An early morning medevac with a military medium sized helicopter was planned. By 0650 we had the injured man to the helispot. At 0900 the helicopter arrived and transported the injured man to Twisp Medical Center and the tender loving care of Doc Henry.

John and I packed up our gear and hiked to Billy Goat Pass and the Eight Mile Trailhead.

After receiving an initial follow up from Doc the injured man was sent to an orthopedic surgeon where the ankle was reconstructed with several screws and a plate. We received word that the cast was done perfectly and the ankle was in perfect alignment. All in all—a tough jump but a good feeling about being able to provide our services. Little did we know that in a few years we would be called upon to make another "fools jump", this time to an injured Missoula jumper with a broken back.

Against All Odds

While on a fire along the Canadian border we found a fragment of a parachute. We concluded that this was left by a 555th Battalion jumper who jumped this very spot in 1945. This inspired me to research and write the following article for the National Smokejumper Association magazine. Used by permission.

"Jumpin the Umpqua old growth with a 50 ft. Letdown rope"

PREFACE

Over the past three decades many articles have been written about the Triple Nickles and Operation Fire Fly. The articles covered both their accomplishments, and their operational issues—a high accident rate and mission inefficiencies. Little was mentioned about the reasons behind the high accident rate and mission inefficiencies. It was not until the Forest Service Final Report did the Forest Service recognize, and take some responsibility for the situation they put the 555th in— Operation Fire Fly was compromised from the beginning. The objective of this paper is to discuss how the Triple Nickles mission was compromised, and how they performed admirably and bravely "Against All Odds."

A FIRE FLY SCENARIO

It's August 10, 1945. The Troop Carrier Command C-47, with 15 Triple Nickle paratroopers aboard, circles over a 20-acre fire in old growth on the Umpqua National Forest. Coming from the flatlands and rolling hills of the south, this is likely the paratroopers' first exposure to the steep mountains and tall conifers of the west.

As the jump ship circles the pilot evaluates the smoke column drift and winds at 1,200 feet AGL and prepares to drop the cargo. He will drop cargo first followed by jumpers. No wind drift chute or drift steamers are used. For all practical purposes the pilot is the spotter.

Equipped with a 28 ft. unmodified camouflage T-7 chute assembly, a military pilot's fleece lined jacket and trousers (or flight suit) with no D-rings, and a 50 ft. letdown rope tied to the harness, the Triple Nickle paratroopers mentally prepare to exit over the 200 plus foot old growth trees.

After dropping the cargo from 1,200 feet, with the "red light" illuminated and static line snap in hand, the jumpers are ordered "stand up" and "hook up" to the overhead cable. A 9-man stick will be the first to jump. On final now, the aircraft is "slowed" to 125 knots and the pilot guides the C-47 to the "guesstimated" exit point. The red light is changed to green, signaling the jumpmaster to drop the stick at 2-second intervals. At 2-second intervals, and 125 knots, the 9 jumpers exit and are scattered over the DZ, a couple beyond the DZ. Some stand no chance of making the intended jump spot and try to avoid landing in the old growth trees by "slipping" their T-7 between the old growth. Those who landed in trees take out their 50-foot letdown ropes and do the best they can to get to the ground safely using the military "reserve chute letdown technique." Now the arduous task of locating the cargo, retrieving it and reassembling the crew to initiate the initial attack.

AUTHOR'S NOTE

In writing this piece I have reviewed several documents including various NSA magazine articles, books written by Fire Fly members of the 555th, independent authors, including Earl Cooley (*Trimotor and Trail*), other authors, and the Army's official Final Report on Project Fire Fly. Although there is a common general account of Operation Fire Fly, there are some differences regarding the training they received, protective gear they were issued, and jump/cargo drop SOPs. The biggest discrepancy is in the jump statistics—number of fires jumped, and number of fire jumps made during the four month activation. Without all of the After Action Reviews it is difficult to verify the actions taken and statistics. I have tried to use what I believe to be the most accurate and reliable information and data.

BACKGROUND

In 1945 the forests of the western United States were facing a potentially severe fire season and were under threat of thousands of Japanese incendiary balloons. NOTE: Army intelligence was aware that no new balloons had arrived over the continent since the middle of April 1945.

The highly acclaimed black 555th Infantry Battalion was trained and ready for action, but without an assignment. President Roosevelt and the military were not willing to send them to the European or Japanese Theaters. Pressed for an assignment in lieu of a combat assignment, the military designed a plan for the Army to provide assistance to civil agencies responsible for combating forest fires which may be caused by incendiary balloons or other causes. The Army offered the services of the 555th to the US Forest Service as part of the military Army Assist Program. The Chief of the Forest Service accepted. There is no indication that US Forest Service Fire Control, or the smokejumper community, requested the 555th to support the smokejumper program. This appears to be a "forced marriage." Politically, this assignment satisfied both President Roosevelt (and wife Eleanor) and the military.

The Fourth Air Force, Western Defense Command and Ninth Service Command, on May 3, 1945, ordered 300 paratroopers from the Triple Nickles to fire duty in the western United States. Their mission would be to counter the Japanese incendiary threat and to fortify the Forest Service smokejumper program. Ironically, there were 220 Forest Service and CPS jumpers, the highest number of jumpers since the program began in 1940. The project was designated Project Fire Fly, officially Operation Fire Fly.

The Triple Nickles reported to Pendleton, Oregon in May 1945. At Camp Pendleton they were given a short course in smokejumping. Forest Service smokejumpers Frank Derry and Jack Allen would serve as instructors. Supporting the project would be a fleet of C-47s from the Air Transport Command (Troop Carrier Command).

After the smokejumper training 100 Triple Nickles were assigned to Chico, California under control of Forest Service Region 5 and 200 remained at Camp Pendleton to serve Forest Service Regions 1,4 and 6.

PUTTING THE 555TH IN PERSPECTIVE

I've tried to put myself in the "jump boots" of the "Triple Nickle rookies." If I were subjected to insufficient fast-tracked "minimal training", inappropriate protective and operational equipment, non-steerable chutes, deficient spotting techniques, and lack operational experience how would I have performed? The project was compromised from the beginning.

I think it's important to put the Fire Fly in perspective. Under the parameters stated in the "Umpqua scenario", would you, or the US Forest Service/BLM programs have performed any better—without modified chutes, with short letdown ropes, exits at +15-25 mph above "normal exit speed", jumps in heavily timbered mountainous terrain without spotters and the aid of drift streamers? Put yourself in their jump boots.

Think back to your rookie training and how the training prepared you for your first fire jump or fire jump in to timber. The following sections discuss what the Triple Nickle jumper was up against— "they jumped against all odds."

"AGAINST ALL ODDS"

SMOKEJUMPER TRAINING

Triple Nickle training consisted of the 40-hour basic military airborne training conducted at Camp Mackall, North Carolina. The final stage of the training consisted of four jumps on flat terrain and one night jump.

After arriving at Camp Pendleton smokejumper specific training commenced on May 22 at Camp Pendleton. Forest Service instructors Frank Derry and Jack Allen conducted a short "smokejumper course." They are the only instructors mentioned. If that's the case, it's hard to determine how much individualized training the 300 trainees received—a very poor instructor to trainee ratio. About the same time, back in Montana, the Forest Service was also training 220 Forest Service and CPS jumpers.

In addition to basic fire behavior and use of fire tools, only a few days were committed to actual jump related training which was supposed to include tree climbing and letdown training without the aid of D-Rings. According to a Triple Nickle interviewed by Chuck Sheley, they were not trained in the Forest Service letdown technique. The Pendleton base was not set up for Forest Service letdown procedure training, and "jump pants" were not modified with the D-Rings. Not confident in the Forest Service training, the Triple Nickle fall back would be to use the military letdown procedure they were more confident in.

The training also included T-7 parachute manipulation into small openings, avoiding trees by using a "slip maneuver." Some sources state that there was an introduction to the Forest Service 28-foot Derry Slotted chute. It is doubtful that they ever made training jumps on the Derry slotted chute. At Pendleton two "flat land" and one timber jump were scheduled. It is very likely that they never made a timber jump.

Jumpmasters, supposedly, received training in techniques for dropping small groups (four men) into virgin timber. There is no indication that the jumpmasters ever got a chance to "spot" the jumpers. The pilot fully controlled the "spotting" and deployment of the jumpers.

The bottom line is—overall the smokejumper training was poor and did not adequately prepare the Triple Nickles for standard smokejumper operations. Part of the problem was the 555ths unwillingness to change from their military methods. In their defense, given that the Forest Service training was fast tracked and trainees likely did not attain full competency in Forest Service specific jumper skills, they had more confidence in their airborne methods than Forest Service methods.

SMOKEJUMPER EQUIPMENT

The Triple Nickle jumpers were provided a minimally protective jump suit. Instead of the standard Forest Service two-piece jump suit, the Triple Nickle was attired with a mix of gear—standard pilot flight suits or a pilot leather cold weather flight jacket and trousers. The protective uniform did not have sewn in D-Rings to facilitate letdowns. There was no pocket for the letdown rope. The letdown rope was tied to the harness.

A standard 50-foot letdown rope was issued. Some reports state 75 ft. ropes were issued and one report states that ropes were as short as 33 feet.

Helmets were modified to include a standard protective metal screen.

PARACHUTES

The standard main parachute was the T-7 28 ft. non-steerable static line (15 ft.) deployed round flat circular canopy. As mentioned, it is doubtful that the 555th ever received instruction on the Derry Slotted 28 ft. canopy. Instruction was given on how to "slip" the T-7 into small openings between the trees.

DEPLOYING THE JUMPERS AND CARGO

Critical to the success of Operation Fire Fly was getting the troops in the DZ and on the ground safely. Also critical to the mission was the deployment of cargo in the DZ where it could be readily retrieved. This proved to be a major program issue on some fires.

The Forest Service offered to instruct the Triple Nickle jumpmasters in Forest Service spotting techniques but the Triple Nickles preferred the military procedures learned at Ft. Benning. The airborne method tasked the jumpmaster to determine the DZ and the pilot to determine the jumper exit point from 1,200 ft. AGL. The Army made it very clear to the Forest Service that they would make the final decision as to whether it was safe to jump. The C-47 pilots were given no special smokejumper related training. No wind indicating devices were used. Estimating the wind direction and velocity along with "smoke observations" helped them to determine the exit point. Sometimes there was a conflict between the pilot and jumpmaster regarding jump conditions and the exit point. Occasionally the jumpmaster would serve as a "test jumper." As a result, spotting was very imprecise and often resulted in scattering the jumpers, especially when standard sticks numbered 5-6, sometimes more jumpers. It is inferred that under some DZ scenarios a stick size may be as large as 10-12 jumpers.

As advisors on fire mission flights both Francis Lufkin and Earl Cooley offered to spot but were turned down. Cooley was told to "stay out of the way." He was to tell them where to jump, but not when! On one flight, after two sticks were badly misspotted, Earl was asked by the pilot "to ring the bell" (spot)— the stick "hit the spot."

The Final Report (US Forest Service) stated that many accidents were attributed to tree landings. The report further stated that the jumpmasters were not sufficiently familiar with mountain and timber conditions to select safe landing areas.

CARGO DROPPING ISSUES

As mentioned, the C-47 Air Transport Command pilots did not receive special smokejumper related training including low level cargo dropping and Forest Service map reading. The cargo drop altitude was from a jump altitude of 1,200 feet AGL before the jumpers were deployed. Some pilots insisted on dropping a large number of cargo packs on a single pass. This resulted in cargo being scattered outside the DZ and making it very difficult to find and retrieve. As a result, fireline operations were delayed while cargo was located and retrieved.

LOGISTICS ISSUES

Other issues negatively affecting the mission were the unavailability of jump aircraft, unavailability of pilots, continual rotation of flight crews making it difficult for pilots to develop proficiency, and lack of parachutes at the time of the jumper request. This resulted in the men being trucked to the fire rather than "jumped."

Of the seven C-47s assigned to the project, 50-70% were normally down for maintenance, or awaiting replacement parts.

For the Pendleton operation the aircraft were stationed at Walla Walla, several miles away. This had an impact on dispatch response time and certainly not conducive for pilot-jumper team building. In Region 5 the jumpers and aircraft were co-located at Chico and there was a much closer relationship between jumpers and flight crews.

HUMAN FACTORS

Most, if not all of the 555th jumpers, were raised in the south or east and did not have "western mountain experience." The steep terrain covered with giant trees was probably quite intimidating. Add to this was the anticipation of a hard opening shock from the exit at 100-125 knots (one report stated 150 mph exit) without a D-bag. Add to this imprecise spotting, a flaming fire front and fear of landing in a tall tree with a short letdown rope, possibly breaking loose and crashing to the ground. The jumper was faced with an extremely emotional challenging experience. Think back to your first fire jump?

Triple Nickle Walter Morris stated: "We know how to jump from airplanes, but the heavily forested areas of the Pacific Northwest presented drop zones that were more difficult and more dangerous than any we had faced before."

EVALUATING THE FIRE FLY PROGRAM

In 1945 the 555th Paratroop Infantry Battalion (Triple Nickle) was assigned to Operation Firefly and fast tracked in to service in the western United States. Insufficiently trained, and poorly equipped, they committed themselves to the task. They wanted to serve their country and this was their opportunity. They were put into a very difficult position with little or no help.

What the Forest Service had accomplished over a six-plus-year period, the 555th had to start with no operational experience. The Triple Nickles were fast tracked into action. The timing of the activation order, with a busy fire season in progress, precluded the number of training days and smokejumper skills that they should have been required to have before committing the 555th to fire operations.

Part of the performance issue was self-inflicted—the Triple Nickle's (Army) reluctance and willingness to adopt Forest Service methods and lessons learned from the Forest Service experience. Adherence to Forest Service SOPs would have improved performance, likely would have reduced the number of injuries and would have improved mission efficiency.

The number of fires jumped, and number of fire jumps made by the Triple Nickles, according to the Army's Final Report, was "15 fires jumped and 444 fire jumps made." The final report was from Neal Rahm of the USFS. Army records are non-existent.

Some unofficial resources stated that 33 fires were jumped and about 1,200 fire jumps made.

Subsequent research concluded that some of these fires that were initially reported as "jumped," were not actually jumped due to lack of jump ships or lack of chutes. The troops were then trucked to the fire. The dispatch record failed to correct the dispatch record from "jumped" to "trucked." The lack of After Action Reviews has made it difficult to verify the actual numbers. Regardless, this is still a significant number of fire jumps. During the four months of activation the 555th sustained 30 significant injuries and one fatality (Malvin Brown).

At the conclusion of Operation Fire Fly the Forest Service made a final report covering both Forest Service Region 5, Chico Operation, and the Pendleton Operation. The Triple Nickle's performance, or value, was both praised, and criticized. The primary criticisms were the high jump injury rate, poor mission efficiency caused by the scattering of jumpers and cargo outside the DZ. Fireline work performance evaluations varied from outstanding to poor. The Region 5 Chico Operation tended to rate their jumpers much higher than Region 1.

Region 5 rated Triple Nickles superior in morale, physical fitness, efficiency and leadership compared to white ground troops. Elmer Neufeld, Okanogan (NCSB) supervisory jumper, worked with the 555th on the Bunker Hill Fire, and gave the Triple Nickles a good fire performance rating. The Forest Service final report stated that "the benefits outweighed the liabilities by a narrow margin."

In the Final Report—Project Fire Fly, the Forest Service took some responsibility for the situation they put the Triple Nickles in. I'm not sure if the Army officially concurred. A few of the Forest Service report comments:

1. Indoctrination should be at least one month.
2. Jumpmasters were not sufficiently familiar with mountainous and timbered country to properly judge safe landing areas and needed a greater familiarity with ground cover in the back country.
3. The 555th should be given more training in jumping in mountainous country.
4. Tendency for the Army (555th) to jump too many men at a time resulting in scattering, especially in fast (C-47) ships. More passes should be made over areas where suitable landing areas are limited.
5. There was a tendency to disregard civilian methods and it was difficult to wean away from Army methods.

Although not specifically mentioned in the Final Report, one report stated that all jumpers should be fully outfitted in standard US Forest Service protective gear.

The Final Report stated that the project "proved to be a valuable asset in strengthening the firefighting forces on the west coast when fire conditions became critical."

Overall, considering the political circumstances of 1945, and the fact that Operation Fire Fly was a "forced marriage," I commend the Triple Nickles for what they endured, how they performed and for their contribution to the forest fire control program during the very busy 1945 fire season. They answered the call and performed the best they could with the hand they were dealt, and performed admirably and bravely— "against all odds!"

Two Fools Jump Again

I guess the confidence gained from the Three Fools escapade gave John and I the confidence to make another "almost night rescue jump"—to Bulldog Mountain, Colville National Forest. The call came in to NCSB at 2015 in mid-July 1985. We were in the middle of staffing fires recently started from a lightning storm that swept through central and northeastern Washington. The Missoula base made an initial attack, from Missoula, on the Bulldog Mountain Fire on the Colville National Forest. One of their jumpers had landed in a 60-foot snag and while attempting a letdown (procedure to rappel to the ground) he missed a step in the procedure and ended up freefalling 30-40 feet to the ground. Initial reports indicated a broken back with lots of pain.

Shortly after receiving the call Volpar N900TH (an Alaskan jump aircraft on detail to NCSB) with spotter Steve Reynaud and jumpers Brent Smith, Jeff Cockerill, Mark Corbett, and EMTs John Button and me took off and headed east. We arrived over the fire area about 2105 and confirmed the approximate location of the injured jumper, Jack Deeds. Reynaud threw streamers and determined there was about 200 yards drift. It was getting pretty dark under the cloud cover. We could make out a stand of 60-80 foot tall lodgepole pine timber and decided to go for the trees. Reynaud guided the Volpar to the exit point. The descent, once again, was quick as we guided our chutes into the trees and hung up.

From a safe altitude the para-rescue gear was dropped. John headed for the injured jumper finding him at the base of the snag. I, along with some of the Missoula jumpers gathered the cargo and moved it to Deeds. We made a preliminary diagnosis that Deeds probably had broken his back although he suffered no loss of limb function or paralysis.

Deeds was put in our modified Stokes litter and transported to the helispot that the Missoula jumpers were preparing a few hundred yards from the scene of the injury. By this time it was 2400 and not safe for a helicopter medevac. Distance precluded a night litter carry to a road. We kept Deeds comfortable over night, I believe with Demerol. At 0451 the Chelan rappel helicopter, 624, landed on the helispot—at 0455 we had Deeds en route to Colville Airport where at 0515 he was transferred to a Life Flight helicopter and taken to Spokane for treatment.

Once again, the team of pilot, spotter and Doc Henry's EMT trained jumpers played a vital role in conducting an efficient and safe rescue—and we were proud to be a part of that team.

Today NCSB continues to maintain a corps of EMTs and para-medics ready to serve their injured bros and others in need— just another example of NCSB's versatility, dedication and commitment to serve. May management recognize this "intangible service" when considering the value and future of NCSB.

Photographs

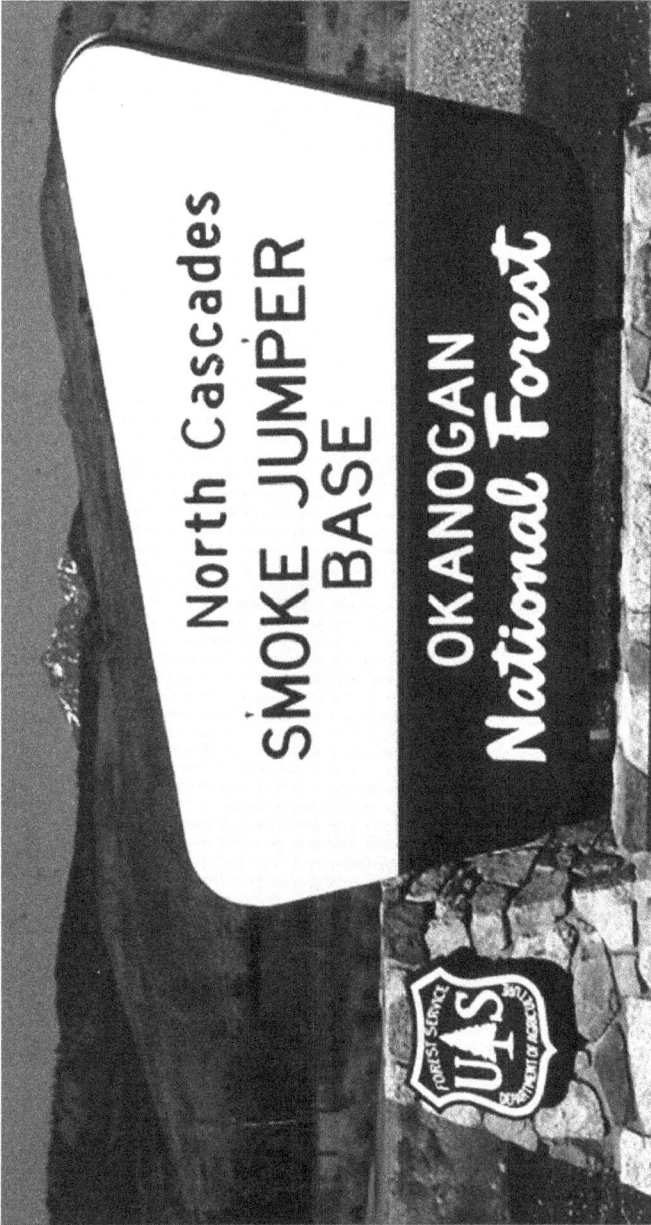

Between Twisp and Winthrop, Washington, on the East County Road.

Colonel Robert Hammerquist, my hero and inspiration.

1957 NCSB rookies Bill Moody, Jack McKay, and Ron Loney.

Exit from a DC-3, similar to many I made.

Bill Moody, Smokejumper, 1957-1989. Photo: Dick Webb.

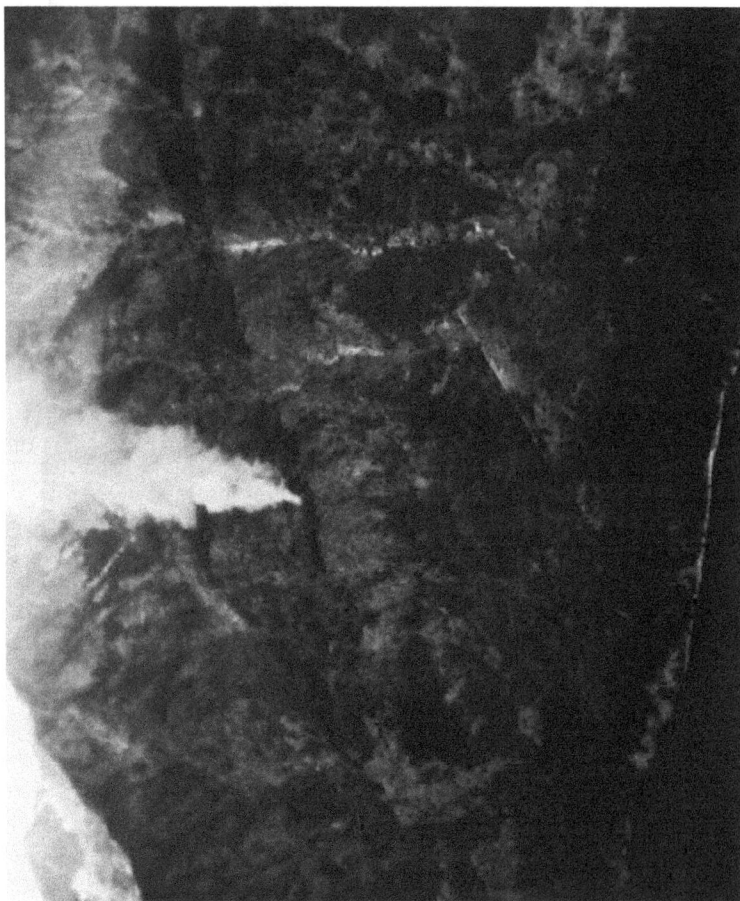

I jumped the Little Creek Fire, Wenatchee National Forest, Chelan Ranger District, September 1970.

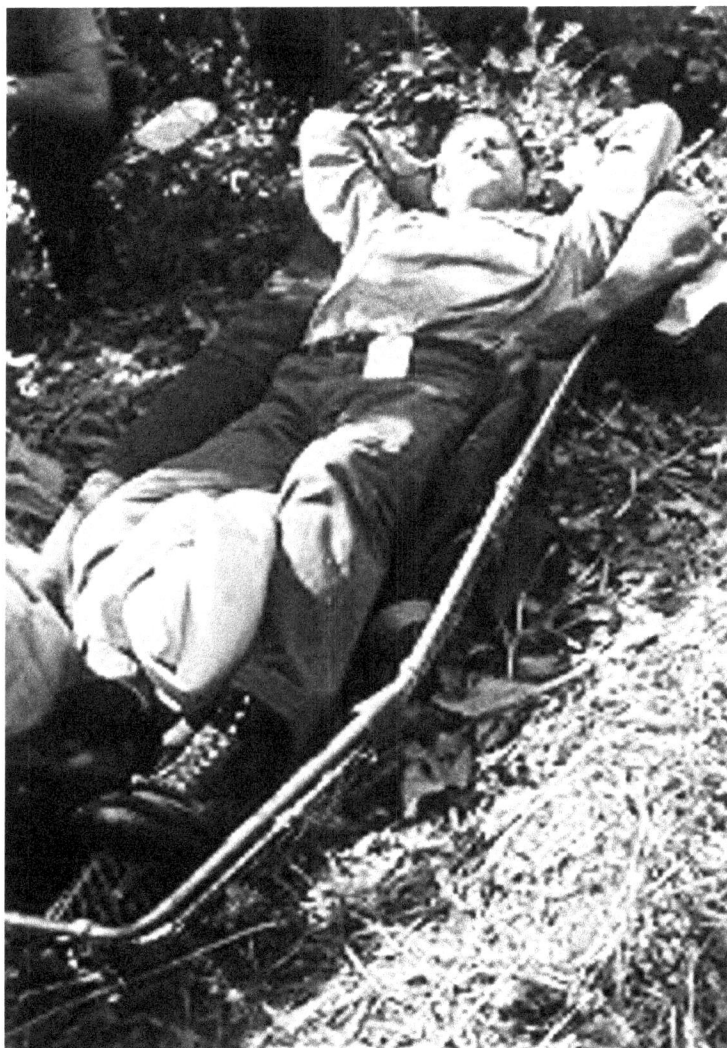

Happy face on a broken femur, August 29th, 1978.

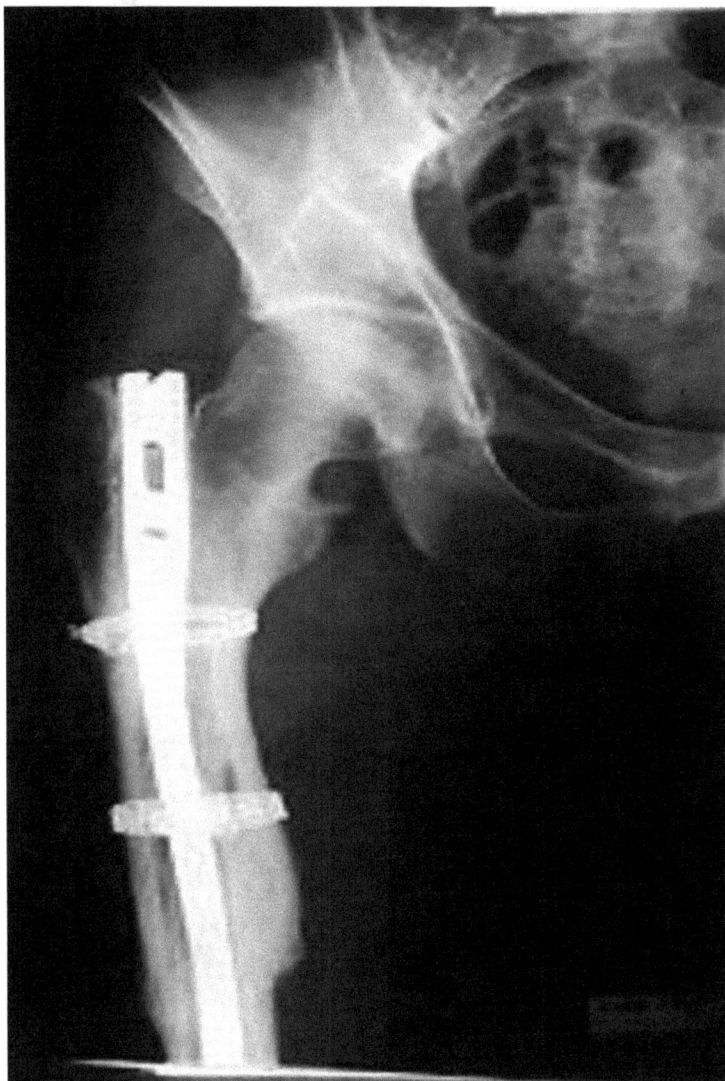

X-ray of the rod attached to my femur.

DC-3 jumping a two-man stick near Silver Star Glacier.

Francis Lufkin's last official act: to spot the NCSB supervisory staff on a hillside east of the base. Francis is at the far right of the photo. I am second from right.

With Russian jumper Nikolai Andreev (L) prior to our historic jump.

I prepare to exit an AN-2 aircraft using Russian chute and gear.

Smokejumpers suited up for the documentary *Smokejumpers: Firefighters from the Sky.* I am at left in Francis Lufkin's 1939 red jump suit. Also pictured: Steve Nemore, Steve Reynaud, Mike Tupper, Eric Hipke.

I make the jump from a Ford Tri-Motor over the Oregon Coast Range, 1998. Still taken from a frame of Stevan Smith's video footage.

Mongolian fire suppression crew I trained in 1998.

Francis and I flanked by two "Triple Nickles" at the Smithsonian Air and Space Museum.

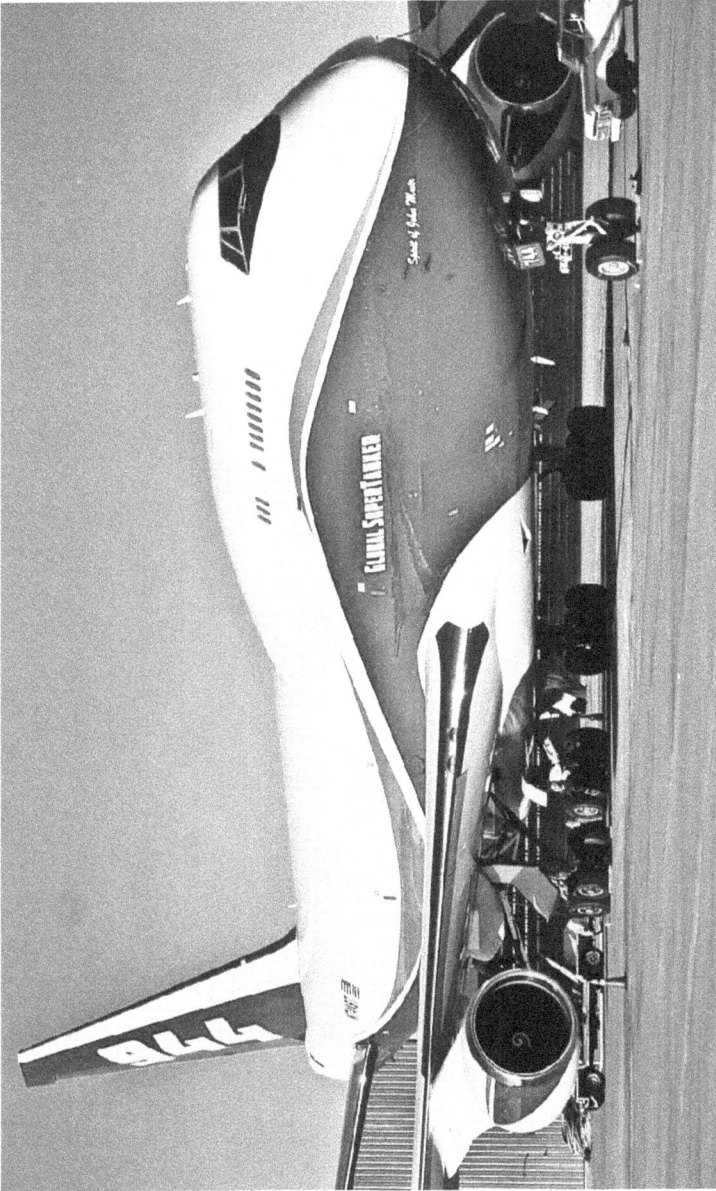

The 747 Supertanker, load capacity of 19,200 gallons.

Demonstrating the Supertanker's value on Israel's Mt. Carmel Fire, 2010.

Jamie Tackman's lead-plane brings in the Supertanker over Chile, 2017.

South of Santiago, Chile, 2017.

With Matt Woosley and the Bolivian lead-plane crew, 2019.

My Air Attack plane, a military G4 Gulfstream flown by the Chilean air force. Call sign *Raptor*.

Acknowledgments

A special thanks to my wife, Sandy, who faithfully accompanied me through my careers, retirements, and adventures, and provided book input and perspective.

Thanks to Soo Ing-Moody for her critical review of Part 1 and her suggestions regarding content and detail. Also to those who challenged me to pursue the various chapters of this sixty-year adventure.

About the Author

In 1956, while still in secondary (high) school, William "Bill" Moody began his sixty-plus-year Fire and Aviation career on a fire crew on the Deschutes National Forest in Central Oregon. Inspired by his World War II paratrooper cousin, in 1957 Bill initiated a thirty-three-year smokejumper career, including eighteen years as Base Manager of the North Cascades Smokejumper Base (NCSB) located in northern Washington State. During the "off-season," he attended college, earning a Master of Education degree. He taught in Wenatchee, Washington, for six years before becoming a full-time U.S. Forest Service Supervisory Smokejumper .

In addition to smokejumping, Bill was certified as an Air Tactical Group Supervisor (Air Attack Officer), Type 3 Incident Commander, and Emergency Medical Technician, parachuting to thirty-one backcountry medical emergencies. After retirement in 1989, Bill continued as a seasonal Air Attack Officer, serving on several Type 1 and 2 Incident Management Teams.

When the 747 Supertanker program was initiated in 2004, Bill was hired as an aerial fire suppression consultant helping to develop the world's largest airtanker. From 2015 until he retired in 2018, he served the program variously as VP, Fire Operations, and Chief of Operations, and continued as an operations "part-timer" through 2021.

Career highlights include making two demo jumps with the Russians in East Siberia as part of the U.S.-Soviet Technical Exchange Program in 1976, training firefighters in Mongolia, and 747 fire assignments in California, Oregon, Israel, Mexico, Bolivia, and Chile.

In 2020 Bill was awarded the prestigious Walt Duran International Aerial Firefighting Award for Aerial Firefighting Safety.

Bill co-authored *Spittin' in the Wind: The Birthplace of Smoke-jumping 1939-2007, Book 1 History and Tales.*

www.ingramcontent.com/pod-product-compliance
Lightning Source LLC
Chambersburg PA
CBHW070558100426

42744CB00006B/325